Two-part — p.126 #6
p.127 #7
#9

C0-AOE-046

Harmonic:
p.237 #4
p.235 #2
p.236 #3

p.110 - #4
p.114 - #2
p.111 - #3
p.118 - [#7] no.2

PRACTICAL EAR TRAINING

JANET McLOUD McGAUGHEY

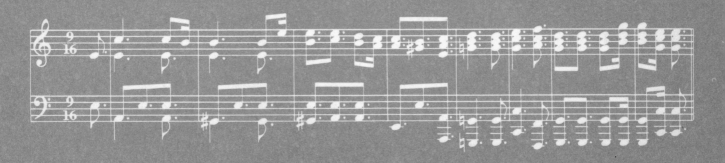

PRACTICAL
EAR TRAINING

JANET McLOUD McGAUGHEY

The University of Texas

PRACTICAL
EAR TRAINING

BOSTON   *Allyn and Bacon, Inc.*   1 9 6 1

Music autographed by Maxwell Weaner

PREFACE

The text and workbook of PRACTICAL EAR TRAINING provide techniques and materials for the systematic cultivation of the musical ear. At a time when there is more and more recognition of the need for intensive ear training in music instruction, this book provides an almost inexhaustible source of training procedures and materials that may be used with a variety of music theory programs in colleges, universities and conservatories. This is evident by the arrangement of PRACTICAL EAR TRAINING chapters according to elements of the fundamental musical vocabulary. The sequence of chapters may be altered according to individual music theory instruction programs, and chapter sections may be divided between earlier and more advanced stages of instruction.

PRACTICAL EAR TRAINING is based on the fundamental principle that the qualified musician must develop reading, singing and notating skills in order to achieve acuity of aural perception and to make effective use of that acuity. Several textbooks dealing wholly or partially with ear training limit their approach to sight singing or to dictation. In each chapter of PRACTICAL EAR TRAINING an extensive variety of activities is provided to insure a complete and integrated command of the particular area of the musical vocabulary involved. Of special value and interest are the *Selective listening* and *Critical listening* sections of each chapter. The student here encounters previously isolated rhythm patterns or sounds in a complete musical context, concentrating on aural recognition in *Selective listening*, and on the combination of visual and aural recognition in *Critical listening*.

An abundance of excerpts from music literature of many periods is contained in nearly all chapters of PRACTICAL EAR TRAINING. After learning to read, perform, and aurally recognize specific patterns and sounds in compact exercises, the student is prepared to identify and notate them as they are found in composed music of larger and more complicated design. The excerpts from music literature provide as well a continual and expansive review of patterns and sounds previously isolated for concentrated study. The excerpts and graded lists of excerpts in several chapters can of course be used in connection with problems emphasized in other chapters. In this way the student is always led to cultivate patterns of response appropriate to actual musical situations.

PRACTICAL EAR TRAINING may serve as the basic text book for a course in ear training, or its materials and techniques may be used in several music theory courses at different levels of undergraduate study. The book is divided into eight chapters with each chapter focusing on one area of the music theory subjects found in nearly all college music curriculums. These subject areas are: rhythm, scales, intervals, melody, two-voice counterpoint, triads, seventh chords, and altered chords.

Each chapter is a complete, self-contained unit with four or more sections that first analyze the components of the chapter topic and then examine their use in various musical contexts. Within each section there is correlated subdivision in terms of the vocabulary involved in both exercise material and composed excerpts. This kind of organization permits the instructor (1) to select a sequence of PRACTICAL EAR TRAINING sections and chapters that best fits the content and level of his particular course or courses, and (2) to find, either within one chapter or among several chapters, different activities and materials of a similar level of difficulty. For instance, a course in fundamentals of music often given at the beginning of a student's freshman year, might involve study of the simple beat with division and easy subdivision and the compound beat with division; the structure of the major scale; and the intervals derived from the major scale. The instructor could select material from each section of Chapters 1, 2 and 3 for immediate use and later introduce the more advanced material from these chapters dealing with further subdivision of the beat; minor, modal and chromatic scales; and augmented and diminished intervals. Such a procedure allows the student from the beginning to engage in interestingly varied learning activities, and to advance from working with exercise material to working with excerpts from music literature.

All students will be able to master the simple material found in each chapter section, as the subject area of each chapter is brought into their theory studies. The more complicated material will offer a challenge to the majority of students; much of it is designed to serve as a basis for understanding and working capably with twentieth century music.

For the music education student and professional teacher, PRACTICAL EAR TRAINING offers an organized program designed to develop the aural acuity necessary to work effectively in public school music. Specifically, the music educator in the elementary classroom will be enabled to record the creative efforts of pupils and to improvise original material and accompaniments for songs and rhythmic activities. For the student preparing for, and teacher engaged in secondary school music teaching, the *Selective listening* and *Critical listening* portions of PRACTICAL EAR TRAINING extensively develop the most important single skill necessary for successfully conducting band, orchestral or choral groups.

For all music students, the book provides ample practice material which may be used outside of the classroom, both individually and in group sessions.

The author is indebted to the following people who have served on the music theory faculty of The University of Texas during the time when the material of this book was being developed and used experimentally: Shirley Lewis Brown, Marian Yeager Luke, Betty Carr Pulkingham, Joan Templar Smith, Phyllis Casselman Young, Andrew J. Broekema, and Jervis Underwood. Thanks are due, also, to Mrs. Luke, Theodore A. Haendschke, and R. Lynn Whitten, whose master's theses provided insight into many of the pedagogical problems involved.

Dean E. William Doty of The University of Texas College of Fine Arts has, through his interest and encouragement, provided ideal circumstances for the preparation and testing of new teaching devices. Miss Elinor Warner's exceptional skill as music editor has contributed materially to the organization of both text and workbook; and finally, Miss Carolyn Kay, Mrs. Roger Wright, and Mrs. Velberta Millerick have been of great assistance in the preparation of the manuscript.

JANET McLOUD McGAUGHEY

Austin, Texas
September, 1960

TABLE OF CONTENTS

INTRODUCTION

1. RHYTHM

2. SCALES

3. INTERVALS

4. MELODY

5. TWO-VOICE COUNTERPOINT

6. TRIADS

7. SEVENTH CHORDS

8. ALTERED CHORDS

PRACTICAL
EAR TRAINING

INTRODUCTION

> This one man, standing alone in the midst of the loud sounds, having the hardest task of all, can discern at every moment if anyone goes astray; and can keep all the musicians in order, restore any waverer to certainty and prevent him from going wrong. Rhythm is in his every limb, he takes in all the harmonies by his subtle ear and utters all the different parts through the medium of his own mouth.[1]

The above description of Johann Sebastian Bach, written by Johann Mathias Gesner, describes the ideal goal for any systematic study in ear training. In the quotation, significant stress is given to the functions of "limb" and "mouth" as well as to the function of ear. In order to train the ear, attention must be devoted not only to aural perception as such, but to reading, writing, singing, and rhythmic movement as well. In addition, the ear-training process will be more effective if the problems are recognized as the kind of problems that are found in practical musical experience. To provide the necessary variety of approaches to ear training, PRACTICAL EAR TRAINING presents a number of different kinds of exercises, each of which focuses on a particular aspect, or combines several aspects, of ear training.

Each chapter (with two exceptions) begins with *Basic drills*, which stress moving, speaking, singing, or visual recognition with regard to the topic of the chapter. Performance is emphasized, so that the student firmly grasps the motion of rhythm patterns or the structure of sonorities encountered in notated form. The patterns read and performed in *Basic drills* will be useful both as preparation for working with the *Selective listening* section of each chapter and for checking the accuracy of notated results. These patterns may be used similarly with the *Dictation* section of many chapters. In Chapter 4, the *Basic drills* consist of short and uniquely designed patterns to be taken down in dictation as preparation for the *Critical listening* and *Dictation* sections of that chapter. Throughout the book, *Basic drills* can be found valuable as preliminary, checking, and remedial material.

---

1 Karl Geiringer, *The Bach Family* (New York: Oxford University Press, 1954), p. 182.

The aim of the *Basic drills* is to provide a vocabulary of response patterns which the student will come to use automatically in reacting to the music he hears. Because of the importance of a complete intellectual grasp of the pattern or sonority being identified by means of the response, it has been necessary to create some *Basic drills* which are quite difficult to perform. Notable among these are the VOCALISES BASED ON CHROMATIC SCALE INTERVALS (Chapter 3), where it is made necessary for the student to call upon his knowledge of the sound of abstract intervals instead of relating the tones to any kind of larger association; and the TRIAD-IN-KEY VOCALISES in Chapter 6, where the harmonic progression is contrary to normal practice, so that the student cannot memorize and "sing by ear" readily but must think each step of the drill carefully.

Selective listening sections are found in nearly every chapter and contribute notably to accuracy in the sight reading and dictation processes. As the name implies, this activity is designed to cultivate the ability to identify and locate a specific rhythm pattern or sonority in a musical context. This involves not only being able to recognize the element sought, but also being able to keep abreast of the forward motion of the musical sounds in order to indicate where that element was heard. *Selective listening* involves using the diagrams provided in the workbook which correspond with musical excerpts appearing in the text. A diagram shows the number of measures in the excerpt and the number of beats within those measures. As the excerpt is played, the student moves his pencil across the diagram in time with the music, placing a check mark on any beat space where he hears the rhythm pattern or sonority for which he is selectively listening. By thus firmly linking movement in time with movement in space on the page, *Selective listening* leads to increased skill in accurate notation during the dictation process. Inability to take down what is heard frequently results from lack of control over the metric placement of symbols rather than from failure to identify the pitches and rhythm patterns heard.

Critical listening sections are found in all chapters and may be described as the technique of correlating musical notation with musical sounds through indicating deviations of sounds heard from the printed notation being followed. The student is asked not only to be aware that an error was made, but to note down exactly what was performed in place of the notated version. This procedure is one of the most effective means of ear training, in that attention is focused on the nature of the error, demanding a response more discriminating than that required in a great deal of practical critical listening as done by teacher, conductor or performer.

There are three outstanding reasons for the prime importance of thorough mastery of the special technique used in *Critical listening*. First, investigation reveals that errors made in reading music tend to fall into certain categories, and by working with carefully constructed drills the student will be taught not only to detect these errors in the performance of others, but to be on guard to avoid them in his own reading. Second, the act of re-notating those portions of the music that differ in the performed version from the notated version encourages the student to follow a notational model with regard to accurate drawing and placement of notation symbols. Finally, and most important, the intense focus on reading demanded for successful completion of *Critical listening* exercises provides for many students a much needed emphasis on accuracy of reading.

Critical listening, like *Selective listening*, involves use of the workbook in conjunction with the text. In the workbook are found rhythmic fragments, scales, intervals, melodies, two-voice counterpoint, chords, and harmonic progressions, all with corresponding blank measures printed beneath them. The same material appears in the text; corresponding measures beneath the original music contain the version to be performed by the instructor or student conducting the drill, a version involving calculated deviations in pitch or rhythm or both. Attention is drawn to the changed notes by arrows; moreover the appearance of the notes is altered through the use of smaller noteheads or shorter stems. Suggested methods for administering *Critical listening* drills appear throughout the text, where needed.

The checking of *Critical listening* exercises in class may be conducted in such a way as to provide counting, singing, and spelling drill in place of a simple verbal discussion of the results. Because of the variation in the material involved, the checking technique will be discussed as needed, and instructors are encouraged to introduce techniques of their own.

Dictation sections consist of excerpts from music literature in most instances, carefully selected for their emphasis of certain rhythm patterns, sonorities, melodic characteristics or harmonic progressions. A classified list of music excerpts drawn from literature found in most music libraries is also provided in many chapters. In addition, instructors and students are urged to draw dictation material from music currently being heard in concerts, performed by individuals in private lessons or in ensemble classes, or studied in music literature courses. In this way examples from less standard sources may also be drawn upon.

Unlike *Selective listening* and *Critical listening*, *Dictation* is an ear training technique familiar to all musicians, and many instructors will wish to follow methods of their own. Some suggestions for procedure are made at certain points in the text and can be easily adapted to prevailing methods.

Sight singing materials and lists are included in later chapters, along with suggestions for use of certain *Basic drills* and *Critical listening* exercises as an aid to greater fluency and accuracy in sight singing. Like *Dictation* material, *Sight singing* material should be drawn whenever possible from music presently heard or being worked with by the student.

Perhaps the most important feature of this text and the accompanying workbook is that they place extensive exercise material and composed music in the hands of the students themselves. Instead of being available only in class or laboratory sessions, purposeful ear-training practice may be carried on at any time by students working alone or in small groups. The student who administers the material, faced with an unremitting demand for accuracy in reading and clarity in performance, benefits fully as much as the students who are taking the drill. Both instructor and student performers are encouraged to use instruments other than the piano whenever this is feasible; in cases where considerable technical proficiency is required, it is best that the performer of the drill use his major instrument.

Constant and intelligent use of the various ear training materials made available here will insure a higher level of aural skill among students whose native talent needs careful cultivation in order that it may be used to its fullest capacity.

CHAPTER 1

Rhythm

Basic drills

The rhythmic *Basic drills* are of two kinds: the Patterns to intone, tap or clap permit the student to rehearse his verbal or
muscular response to rhythmic notation through exercises introduc-
ing a few problems at a time; the Ensemble drills to intone, tap,
or clap present similar problems in two- and three-part combinations. In order to clarify the relationship between these drills and
those in later sections of this chapter, the organization is by subject
matter and is not necessarily by order of difficulty.

The first three sets of Patterns to intone, tap, or clap deal
with the simple beat (the beat whose basis division is into two
parts). The first set introduces the division of the simple beat into
two and four parts. Meter signatures are used which produce duple,
triple, and quadruple meter, and half, quarter, and eighth notes as
units of beat. Sextuple simple meter may be rehearsed with the
exercises provided for duple compound meter. The next two sets
take up the simple beat subdivided and the simple beat with triplets and sextuplets.

The last three sets of Patterns to intone, tap, or clap involve
the compound beat (the beat whose basic division is into three
parts). The first set deals with the division of the compound beat
into three and six parts. Meter signatures are used which produce
duple, triple, and quadruple meter, and dotted half, dotted quarter,
and dotted eighth notes as units of beat. The last two sets take up
the compound beat subdivided and the compound beat with duplets
and quadruplets.

Various meters are used to familiarize the student with combinations of simple and compound beats resulting from introduction of
triplets and sextuplets in simple time, and of duplets and quadruplets in compound time. Because of the comparative rarity of occur-
rence of meters such as quintuple and septuple and of beat divisions
such as quintuplets and septuplets, it has not been felt necessary to
create special exercises to rehearse these problems. The same is

true of the small subdivisions, such as the eight-part subdivision of the simple beat, and of the use of whole notes and sixteenth notes as units of beat.

The average student reads rhythm more easily if the unit of beat is a dotted or an undotted quarter note. In order that he may learn to read more readily when the unit is the less familiar half note or eighth note, dotted and undotted, each pattern will be notated three times in succession. This permits the student to perform each pattern three times, adjusting to a new notational framework each time.

These drills are to be intoned with a neutral syllable such as *da* or with any system of rhythmic counting prescribed by the instructor. In addition to intoning the patterns the student is encouraged to tap or clap them; he may tap with the left hand while keeping the conductor's beat with the right, or clap the patterns while saying the beats or tapping them with the foot. All of these methods, and any others which are feasible, should be used in order to gain facility, accuracy, and freedom in rhythmic intonation and movement.

The remaining *Basic drills* are ENSEMBLE DRILLS TO INTONE, TAP OR CLAP, arranged according to rhythmic vocabulary. These will involve two or more individuals or groups in the class, and a student or the instructor may serve as conductor if desired. Like the preceding PATTERNS TO INTONE, TAP, OR CLAP, these drills take up first the simple beat with its divisions and subdivisions and then similarly the compound beat. Individual students may use the two-part exercises for rhythmic independence drills, tapping one part with each hand or saying one part while tapping or clapping the other.

Classes and student practice sessions may proceed with rhythmic ensemble drills drawn from music literature, especially from small ensembles involving string or wind instruments. For example, it is a stimulating exercise for four students to arrange themselves in string quartet formation with music stands before them, and then perform the rhythms of the individual parts of a quartet. If possible the other students observing should have full scores to follow so that they may practice "critical listening." This type of experience is especially important for the singer or the keyboard performer to whom it brings insight into the demands of instrumental ensemble. A list of works suitable for such treatment appears at the end of this section.

PATTERNS TO INTONE, TAP, OR CLAP

1. SIMPLE BEAT DIVIDED

(a)

(b)

(c)

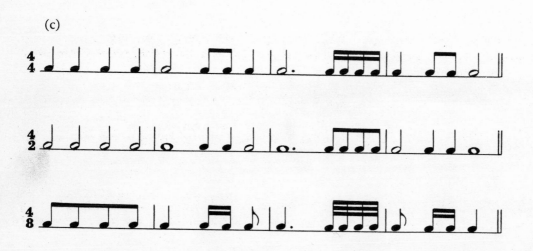

2. SIMPLE BEAT SUBDIVIDED

(a)

(b)

(c)

3. SIMPLE BEAT WITH TRIPLETS AND SEXTUPLETS

(a)

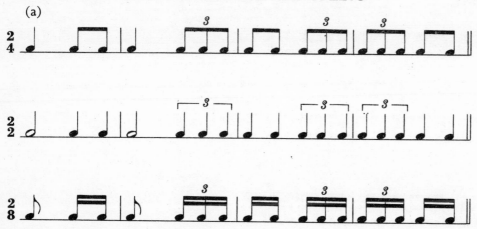

(b)

(c)

4. COMPOUND BEAT DIVIDED

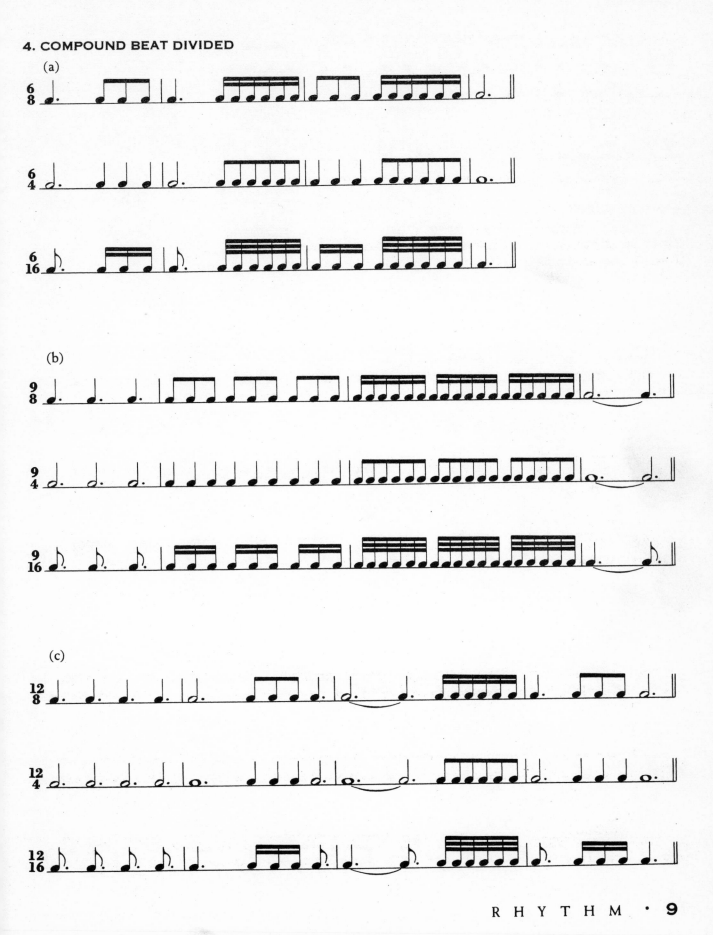

(d)

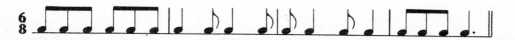

(e)

(f)

5. COMPOUND BEAT SUBDIVIDED

(a)

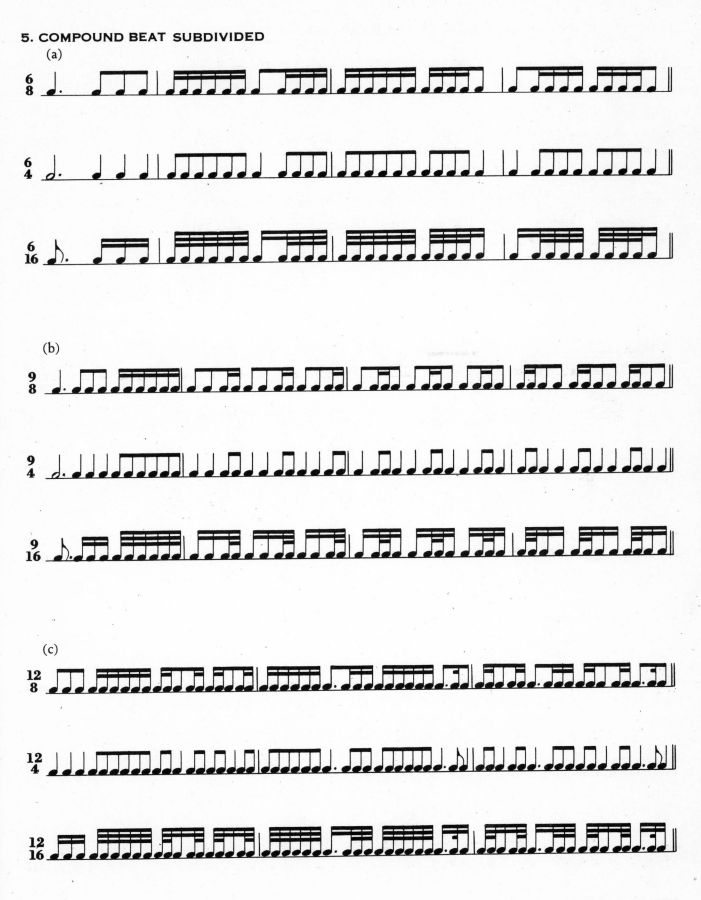

(b)

(c)

Basic drills

6. COMPOUND BEAT WITH DUPLETS AND QUADRUPLETS

(a)

(b)

(c)

ENSEMBLE DRILLS TO INTONE, TAP, OR CLAP

1. SIMPLE BEAT DIVIDED

(a)

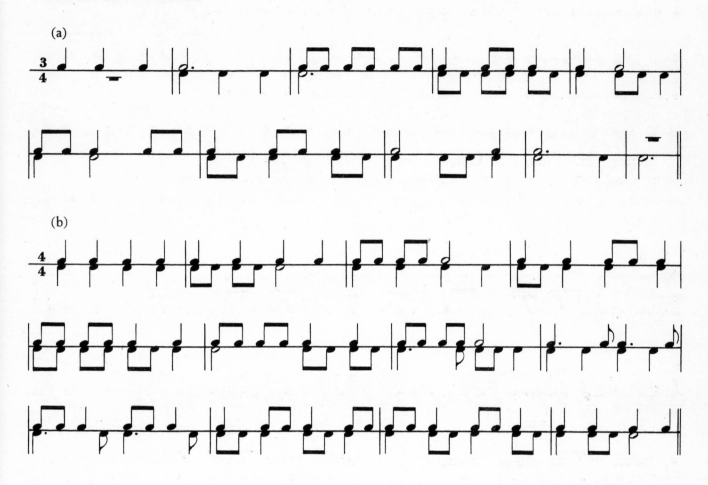

2. SIMPLE BEAT SUBDIVIDED

(a)

(b)

(c)

(d)

(e)

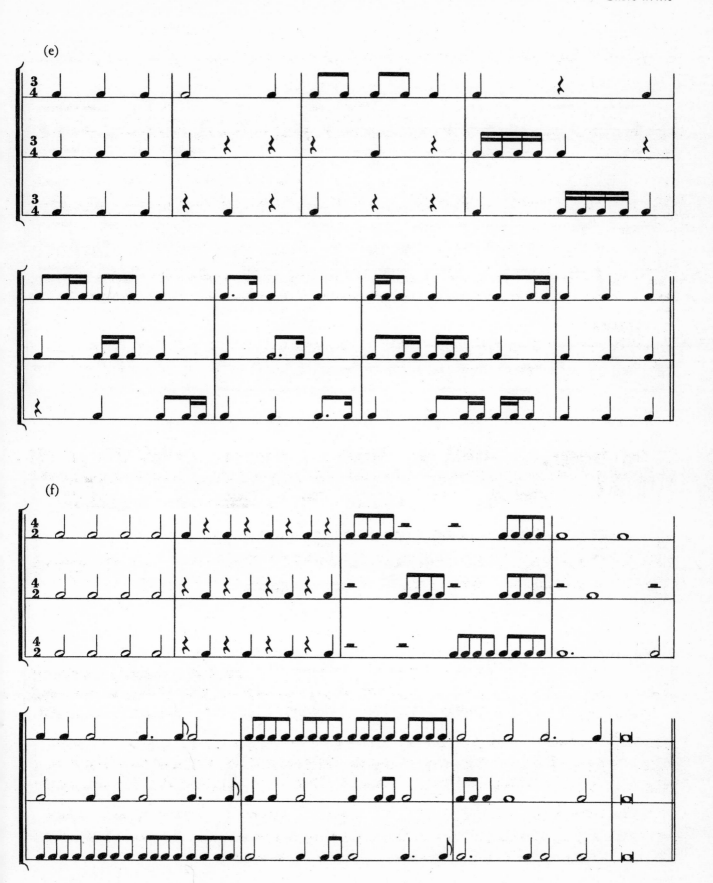

3. SIMPLE BEAT WITH TRIPLETS

(c)

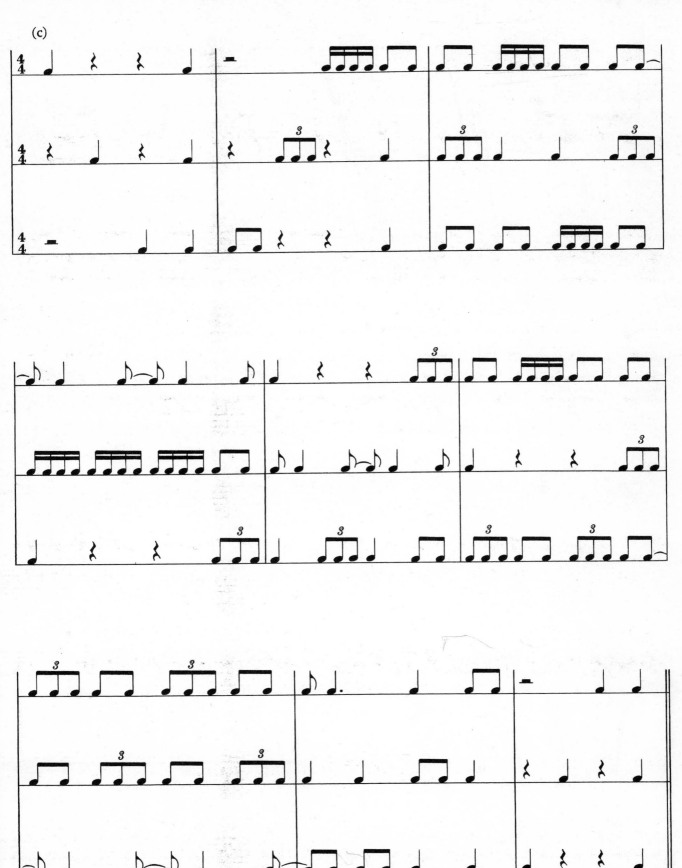

4. SIMPLE BEAT WITH EXTENSIVE SYNCOPATION

(a)

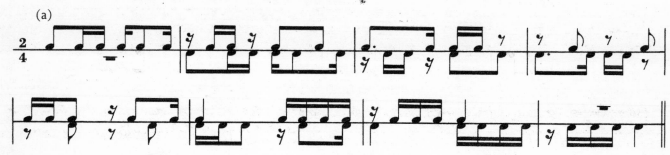

(b)

(c)

5. COMPOUND BEAT DIVIDED

(a)

(b)

6. COMPOUND BEAT SUBDIVIDED

7. COMPOUND BEAT WITH DUPLETS AND QUADRUPLETS

(a)

(b)

8. COMPOUND BEAT WITH EXTENSIVE SYNCOPATION

LIST OF ENSEMBLE DRILLS FROM LITERATURE

1. Simple beat divided
   A. Easy:
      (1) Beethoven: String Quartet, Op. 18, No. 3, third movement
      (2) Beethoven: String Quartet, Op. 18, No. 4, second movement (brief occurrence of subdivision)
      (3) Beethoven: String Quartet, Op. 18, No. 5, second movement
   B. Difficult:
      (1) Beethoven: String Quartet, Op. 18, No. 1, third movement
      (2) Beethoven: String Quartet, Op. 59, No. 1, second movement (brief occurrence of subdivision)
      (3) Beethoven: String Quartet, Op. 18, No. 6, third movement, Scherzo only (extensive syncopation)
      (4) Verdi: *Requiem*, Sanctus, mm. 9-79 (8-part drill — double chorus)

2. Simple beat subdivided
   A. Easy:
      (1) Mozart: String Quartet, K. 387, second movement
      (2) Beethoven: String Quartet, Op. 18, No. 1, first movement
      (3) Beethoven: String Quartet, Op. 18, No. 5, fourth movement
      (4) Purcell: *Dido and Aeneas*, No. 11, "To the Hills and the Vales"
      (5) Bach: *Magnificat*, Opening Chorus (five parts)
      (6) Handel: *Messiah*, "Let Us Break Their Bonds Asunder"
   B. Difficult:
      (1) Beethoven: String Quartet, Op. 18, No. 3, second movement
      (2) Bach: *St. Matthew Passion*, No. 15, chorus section, "Lord, Is It I?"
      (3) Bach: *Magnificat*, No. 7, "Fecit Potentiam" (five parts)
      (4) Handel: *Messiah*, "Blessing and Honor" (four parts)
      (5) Haydn: *The Creation*, No. 27b, "Achieved Is the Glorious Work"
      (6) Haydn: String Quartet, Op. 76, No. 5, fourth movement

3. Compound beat divided
   A. Easy:
      (1) Beethoven: String Quartet, Op. 131, second movement
      (2) Bach: *St. Matthew Passion*, opening chorus, "Come, Ye Daughters" (double chorus with solo provides 9-part drill if desired)
      (3) Bach: *Magnificat*, No. 12, "Gloria" (five parts) mm. 1-15
   B. Difficult:
      (1) Beethoven: String Quartet, Op. 18, No. 3, fourth movement
      (2) Haydn: String Quartet, Op. 1, No. 6, first movement
      (3) Haydn: String Quartet, Op. 33, No. 2, fourth movement

4. Compound beat subdivided
   A. Easy:
      (1) Mozart: String Quartet, K. 421, fourth movement, mm. 1-48, 97-142
      (2) Beethoven: String Quartet, Op. 59, No. 2, first movement
      (3) Beethoven: String Trio, Op. 9, No. 3, third movement
   B. Difficult:
      (1) Mozart: String Quartet, K. 421, fourth movement, mm. 49-96

(2) Beethoven: String Quartet, Op. 18, No. 1, second movement.
(3) Beethoven: String Quartet, Op. 127, second movement, mm. 1-38 (extensive syncopation)

5. Simple and compound beats in combination
   A. Easy:
      (1) Mozart: String Quartet, K. 464, first movement
      (2) Beethoven: String Quartet, Op. 18, No. 2, third movement
      (3) Verdi: *Requiem*, Lux Aeterna, mm. 15-53
   B. Difficult:
      (1) Mozart: String Quartet, K. 421, first movement
      (2) Beethoven: String Quartet, Op. 18, No. 1, fourth movement (some quintuplets also)
      (3) Beethoven: String Quartet, Op. 18, No. 2, first movement
      (4) Beethoven: String Quartet, Op. 18, No. 3, first movement

Selective listening

The general nature of the *Selective listening* process has been discussed in the Introduction. In listening selectively for characteristic rhythmic patterns within the beat, the student will need to be clearly aware of the sound for which he is listening and to feel the tempo so as to move across the diagrammed measures in time with the established beat. Two preliminary drills are recommended: first, establish the tempo and say the rhythmic pattern in question several times in tempo; second, count the beats out loud while tapping the corresponding places on the diagram. As soon as he has gained sufficient proficiency the student may discard these preliminaries.

This section is divided into two parts. The first deals with the simple beat and its subdivisions; the second, with the compound beat and subdivisions.

As the instructor or a fellow student plays the melodic fragment in this book which corresponds with a diagram on the work sheets, the student must be careful to move across the diagram in tempo so as to place check marks on the precise beats where he hears the rhythmic pattern for which he is listening.

After a group of patterns has been completed, either in class or in a practice session, it is profitable to check the papers together in order to determine the nature and probable cause of errors, especially in cases where beats were checked which did not contain the pattern being isolated.

Where the melodic fragment used begins with an upbeat, the rhythmic notation of the upbeat appears on the diagram in order to avoid confusion. Since reading practice is not involved, only the quarter and dotted quarter notes are used as the unit of beat for notating the patterns.

Many of the melodic fragments included in this section may be used for drilling two or more different rhythm patterns. Additional rhythm patterns are shown in parenthesis above excerpts and two diagrams are provided for each selection. The listener may also aurally compare various indicated rhythm patterns after identifying and locating one rhythm pattern on the worksheet. In this way a continual review hearing of patterns previously emphasized may be achieved.

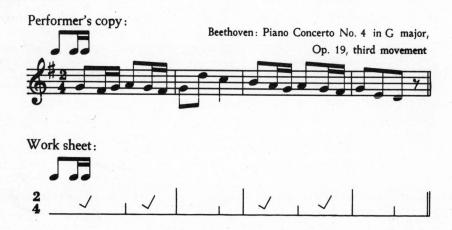

SIMPLE BEAT

COMPOUND BEAT

Unit of Beat

Beat division patterns

1.

Presto — Haydn: Symphony No. 100

(a)

Andante grazioso — Beethoven: Six Bagatelles, Op. 33, No. 1

(b)

2.

Allegro — Mozart: Piano Concerto in B♭ major, K. 450, third movement

(a)

Poco allegro — Brahms: String Sextet No. 2 in G major, Op. 36, fourth movement

(b)

6. Brahms: Sonata No. 1 in G major for violin and piano, Op. 78, first movement

a) Vivace ma non troppo

b) Allegretto — Chopin: Nocturne in B major, Op. 9, No. 3

7. Brahms: Intermezzo in E♭ major, Op. 117, No. 1

a) Andante moderato

b) Andante — Mendelssohn: Violin Concerto in E minor, Op. 64, second movement

8. Handel: *Messiah*, No. 13, "Pastoral Symphony"

a) Allegretto

b) Andantino — Bizet: *Carmen*, Chorus of Cigarette Girls

Critical listening

It is not feasible to include a section involving the simplest type of rhythm in the *Critical listening* drills. If, for example, all subdivisions of the beat were excluded, the possibility for reasonably predictable errors in performance would be so limited as to offer very little material for drill. It is entirely practical, however, to arrange the exercises in order of increasing difficulty on the basis of the familiarity and unfamiliarity of the meter signatures and rhythmic patterns used. It is a well-known fact that patterns read with ease when the quarter note is the unit of beat present a considerable obstacle when based on the half note or eighth note unit. It will be noticed that as a further test of the students' alertness a few exercises are performed exactly as notated.

The *Critical listening* exercises are of two types. The first group, EXERCISES WITHOUT PITCH, consists of rhythm patterns to be performed on one tone, so that no problem of pitch will interfere. These are divided into patterns involving the simple beat and patterns involving the compound beat. The second group, EXERCISES WITH PITCH, is made up of rhythm patterns combined with a melodic line. These are again divided into sections on the simple beat and the compound beat. Within each section, the exercises are arranged from less to more difficult. The compound beat sections include examples where an entire measure is to be treated as a single beat.

Matters such as tempo, number of playings, and medium of performance for the exercises without pitch (tapping, playing a single tone on the piano, etc.) must be left up to the instructor or student administering the drill, to be determined on the basis of the experience and competence of the students involved. Certain suggestions are offered here, however, in order to indicate how a maximum number of skills may be brought into play in a critical listening drill:

1. Except in the few cases which involve no errors, the person giving the drill does not perform the exercise in its original form since this would defeat the primary purpose of teaching the student to hear what he sees. The performer may, however, establish the tempo and allow the class to read the rhythm through silently.

2. During the first hearing of the altered exercise the student is advised to make a check mark or draw a line under the given pattern when the performance is at variance with what he sees.

3. During subsequent hearings and by recalling what was performed, the student enters, in the corresponding measures on the line below, the notation of what was performed in those places which differed from the original. It is not necessary to recopy the portions which correspond with the original.

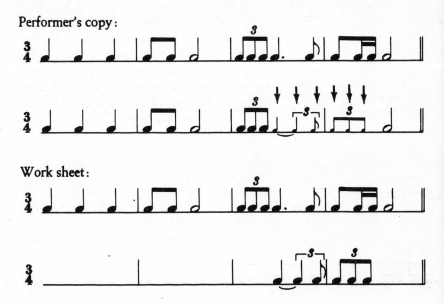

Performer's copy:

Work sheet:

4. If the material is being checked in class, the checking process may be made to serve as a rhythmic counting and rhythmic notation drill as follows:

a. The instructor plays the altered version.

b. An individual or the class repeats the pattern, using a neutral syllable or one of the counting systems recommended by various theory texts.

c. The same individual, another individual, or the class then reads the original rhythm.

d. The instructor calls on a student to discuss the notation of the portions at variance with the original.

As in the case of *Selective listening*, these same exercises may be re-used for additional practice material. In *Critical listening* the performer may substitute other errors for those given in the book. For example, Exercise 6 on page 40 may be performed:

In re-using the work sheets the student may write above or below the first altered version or may place a fresh sheet of paper alongside the original version and sketch in the diagrammed measures.

Throughout the entire course of study the student must bear in mind that completed *Critical listening* drills are an important source of practice material. The comparison of that which was seen with that which was heard — with special emphasis on places where the student was in error — provides an opportunity for cultivating greater precision in reading, in writing, and in hearing. The student should compare the two versions by performing them in every way appropriate to the problem, such as counting, singing, and playing.

EXERCISES WITHOUT PITCH

1. SIMPLE BEAT

(11)

(12)

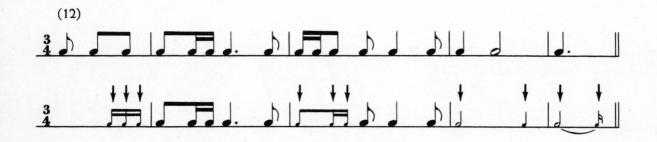

(13)

(More difficult meter signatures and rhythm patterns)

(14)

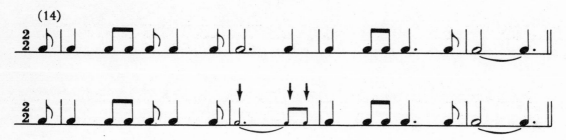

(15)

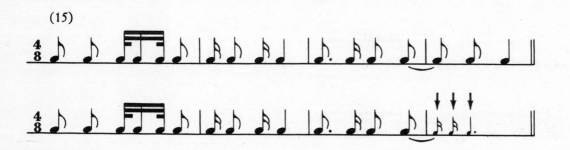

(16)

(17)

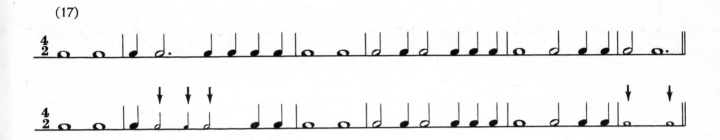

(18)

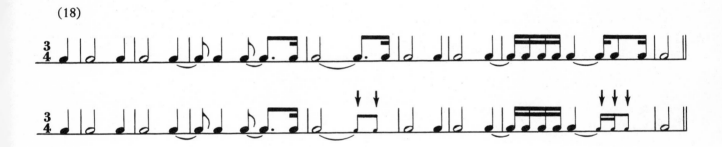

(19)

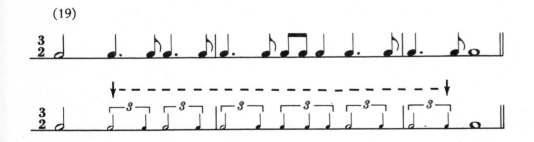

(20)

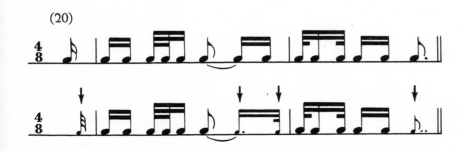

2. COMPOUND BEAT

(6)

(7)

(8)

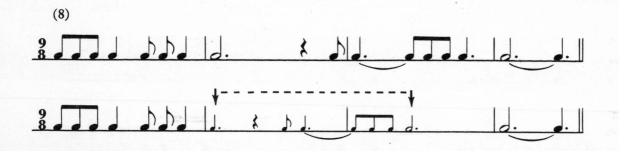

(9)

(10)

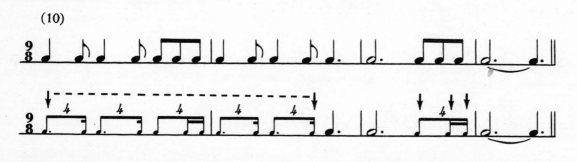

(11)

(12)

(More difficult meter signatures and rhythm patterns)

(13)

(14)

(15)

Critical listening

(16) One beat per measure

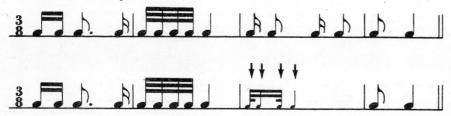

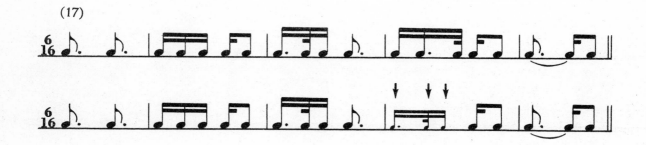

(17)

(18)

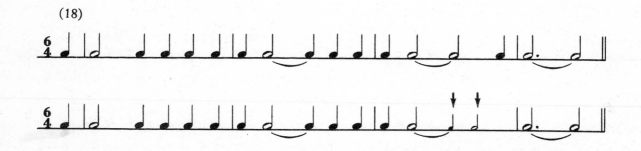

(19)

(20)

(21)

(22)

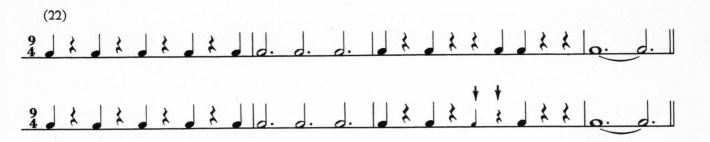

(23)

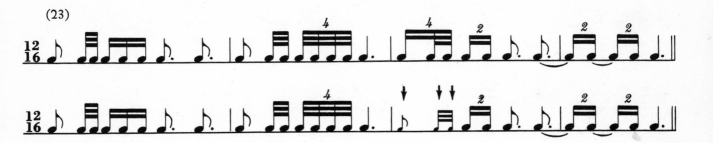

(24)

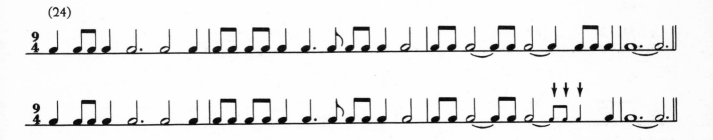

(25) One beat per measure

EXERCISES WITH PITCH

1. SIMPLE BEAT

(More difficult meter signatures and rhythm patterns)

2. COMPOUND BEAT

(5)

(More difficult meter signatures and rhythm patterns)

(6)

(7)

(8)

(9)

(10)

(11) One beat per measure

Dictation

In the dictation process all of the skills previously isolated and drilled are brought into play: the patterns rehearsed in the *Basic drills* are identified; their location is fixed, and a sense of forward motion is maintained through the technique achieved in *Selective listening*, and precision in representing the rhythmic sounds in notation will be achieved through the kind of constant evaluation process cultivated in *Critical listening*. The organization of the EXCERPTS FROM LITERATURE follows closely that of the preceding sections, dealing first with the simple beat and then with the compound beat.

The amount of preliminary information given the class or practice group and the number of playings of the dictation problem will depend on the students' proficiency. In the early stages a preliminary hearing of the problem followed by discussion of and agreement on the type of meter, type of beat, available meter signatures, and number of measures, will be effective. It is imperative that the dictation process itself be a genuine musical performance. This can be assured through the use of phonograph recordings. If the instructor or a student performs, careful attention must be paid to correct tempo, phrasing, and articulation.

The process of checking and correcting work may be itself a rhythmic performance, with one student reading his version rhythmically and other students isolating any errors with the type of response employed in *Critical listening*.

The excerpts for dictation and the list of rhythmic dictation from literature may be supplemented with the list appearing at the end of Chapter 4, since that list is provided with code numbers indicating the rhythmic nature of the melodies cited. As was recommended in the Introduction, a primary source of rhythmic dictation material should be found in music with which the student is concerned in other musical activities in order to increase his receptivity and understanding.

It will be noted that the list is further augmented by reference to melodies found in the *Selective listening* section of this chapter.

LIST OF DICTATION FROM LITERATURE

1. Simple beat divided
   A. Clear duple, triple, or quadruple meter:
      (1) Brahms: Waltz, Op. 39, No. 1 (piano) mm. 1-8
      (2) Dvorak: Slavonic Dance, Op. 46, No. 1 (orchestra) mm. 1-8
      (3) Tschaikovsky: Symphony No. 5, third movement, mm. 1-8
      (4) Beethoven: Piano Sonata, Op. 7, third movement, mm. 1-8 or 1-24
   B. Unusual or shifting meter:
      (1) Prokofieff: Piano Concerto No. 3, third movement, mm. 1-9
      (2) Arr. Martin Shaw: "Righteous Joseph," Oxford Book of Carols, No. 41
      (3) Mussorgsky: *Pictures at an Exhibition* (piano or orchestra) Opening Promenade

2. Simple beat subdivided
   A. Clear duple, triple, or quadruple meter:
      (1) Haydn: String Quartet, Op. 76, No. 3, third movement, mm. 1-20
      (2) Tschaikovsky: *Nutcracker Suite*, "Trepak," mm. 1-16
      (3) Beethoven: Piano Sonata, Op. 2, No. 3, first movement, mm. 1-8
      (4) Bach: French Suite No. 6, Polonaise, mm. 1-8
      (5) *Selective listening*, SIMPLE BEAT, 2 and 4a (page 25)
   B. Unusual or shifting meter:
      (1) Bartok: Rumanian Folk Dances (piano), No. 5

C. More difficult subdivision
  (1) Kodály: *Háry János* Suite, Op. 15, "Intermezzo," mm. 5-8
  (2) Bach: French Suite No. 2, Sarabande, mm. 1-8
  (3) Prokofieff: "March" from *Love of the Three Oranges* (as many measures as desired)
  (4) *Selective listening*, SIMPLE BEAT, 4b (page 26)

3. Simple beat with compound subdivision
  A. Clear duple, triple, or quadruple meter
    (1) Bach: *Mass in B minor*, No. 22, Benedictus, opening violin solo, mm. 1-12
    (2) Honegger: *King David*, No. 27, "The Death of David," mm. 13-25
  B. Unusual or shifting meter
    (1) Tschaikovsky: Symphony No. 6, second movement, mm. 1-8
    (2) Honegger: *King David*, No. 6, "In the Lord I Put My Faith"

4. Simple beat with Ties and Syncopation
  (1) Franck: Sonata in A major, violin and piano, second movement, mm. 14-23
  (2) Beethoven: *Coriolan Overture*, mm. 15-20
  (3) Bach: Well-tempered Clavier, Book II, Fugue in E minor, mm. 1-6
  (4) *Selective listening*, SIMPLE BEAT, 3, 5, 6, and 7 (pages 25-26)

5. Compound beat divided
  (1) Schumann: Album for the Young, Op. 68, *Sicilienne*, mm. 1-8
  (2) Beethoven: Violin Concerto in D major, Op. 61, third movement, mm. 1-8
  (3) Scarlatti: Sonata in E, Longo 430, mm. 1-4
  (4) *Selective listening*, COMPOUND BEAT, 1, 2b, and 3b (pages 27-28)

6. Compound beat subdivided
  (1) Handel: *Messiah*, "How Beautiful Are the Feet" (as many measures as desired)
  (2) Haydn: Song: "My Mother Bids Me Bind My Hair" (as many measures as desired)
  (3) Bach: Well-tempered Clavier, Book I, Fugue in G major, mm. 1-4
  (4) *Selective listening*, COMPOUND BEAT, 2a, 4, 5, 7, 9, 11a, 13 (pages 27-31)
  (5) Schubert: *Mass in G*, Benedictus, mm. 4-19
  (6) Haydn: *The Creation*, No. 9, "With Verdure Clad" (as many measures as desired)
  (7) Haydn: *The Creation*, No. 22, "Straight Opening Her Fertile Womb," mm. 40-54 (melody alternately in accompaniment and solo)
  (8) Beethoven: Piano Sonata, Op. 22, second movement, mm. 1-9
  (9) *Selective listening*, COMPOUND BEAT, 3a, 8, 10, 12 (pages 28-31) more difficult

7. Compound beat with ties and syncopation
  A. Clear, duple, triple, or quadruple meter
    (1) Beethoven: Piano Sonata, Op. 109, second movement, mm. 1-16
    (2) *Selective listening*, COMPOUND BEAT, 3, 5, 6, 8, 9, 10b, 11b, 12, 14 (pages 28-31)
  B. Unusual or shifting meter
    (1) Brahms: Symphony No. 3 first movement, mm. 3-13

EXCERPTS FROM LITERATURE

1. SIMPLE BEAT DIVIDED

Allegro — Haydn: String Quartet in C major, Op. 76, No. 3, third movement

Andante moderato ma con moto — Bizet: *L'Arlésienne*, Suite No. 2, "Intermezzo"

2. SIMPLE BEAT SUBDIVIDED

Presto — Haydn: String Quartet in F major, Op. 74, No. 2, fourth movement

Tschaikovsky: *Nutcracker Suite*, "Dance of the Sugar Plum Fairy"

Andante cantabile — Mozart: Symphony No. 41 in C major, ("Jupiter"), second movement

Adagio — Beethoven: Symphony No. 4 in B♭ major, second movement

3. SIMPLE BEAT WITH TRIPLETS AND SEXTUPLETS

Schumann: Symphony No. 4 in D minor, second movement

Ziemlich langsam

Andante cantabile

Mozart: Symphony No. 41 in C major, ("Jupiter"), second movement

4. SIMPLE BEAT WITH TIES AND SYNCOPATION

Allegro

Beethoven: Leonore Overture, No. 3

Bach: Concerto in D minor for clavier

5. COMPOUND BEAT DIVIDED

Andante moderato

Brahms: Symphony No. 4 in E minor, second movement

Allegro assai

Beethoven: Sonata in C major, Op. 2, No. 3, fourth movement

6. COMPOUND BEAT SUBDIVIDED

Andante

Mozart: *The Marriage of Figaro*, Act IV, "Deh vieni non tardar"

Allegro grazioso

Brahms: Symphony No. 3 in F major, first movement

Bach: *St. Matthew Passion*, "Have Mercy, Lord, On Me"

Largo

tr

7. COMPOUND BEAT WITH TIES AND SYNCOPATION

Beethoven: Symphony No. 7 in A major, first movement

Vivace

Allegro

Brahms: Symphony No. 1 in C minor, first movement

CHAPTER 2

Scales

Basic drills

The *Basic drills* on scales are naturally concerned with singing, since the ability to recognize a scale pattern heard is considerably fostered by being able to produce that sound vocally.

The *Basic drills* are divided into two parts. The first deals with the familiar scale forms — the major and minor scales. It includes vocalises on ascending and descending scales, drills with emphasis on the upper tetrachord, and drills with emphasis on the specific intervallic content of these familiar scale forms.

The second group of vocalises, involving unfamiliar scale forms, permits the student to become acquainted with the structure and sound of the medieval modes in a manner that relates them to the more familiar forms previously drilled. The chromatic and whole-tone scales which conclude the set provide practice in intonation. Spelling drill may be coupled with singing by choosing a variety of starting pitches and singing the vocalises with letter names.

VOCALISES ON MAJOR AND MINOR SCALE FORMS

1. ASCENDING AND DESCENDING SCALES

2. EMPHASIS ON UPPER TETRACHORDS

3. EMPHASIS ON INTERVALLIC CONTENT

Major

1　2　Ma - jor　se - cond　2　3　Ma - jor　se - cond　3　4　Mi - nor　se - cond

4　5　Ma - jor　se - cond　5　6　Ma - jor　se - cond　6　7　Ma - jor　se - cond

7　1　Mi - nor　se - cond　1　7　Mi - nor　se - cond　7　6　Ma - jor　se - cond　6　5　Ma - jor　se - cond

5　4　Ma - jor　se - cond　4　3　Mi - nor　se - cond　3　2　Ma - jor　se - cond　2　1　Ma - jor　se - cond

Pure Minor

1　2　Ma - jor　se - cond　2　3　Mi - nor　se - cond　3　4　Ma - jor　se - cond

4　5　Ma - jor　se - cond　5　6　Mi - nor　se - cond　6　7　Ma - jor　se - cond

7　1　Ma - jor　se - cond　1　7　Ma - jor　se - cond　7　6　Ma - jor　se - cond　6　5　Mi - nor　se - cond

5　4　Ma - jor　se - cond　4　3　Ma - jor　se - cond　3　2　Mi - nor　se - cond　2　1　Ma - jor　se - cond

Melodic Minor

Harmonic Minor

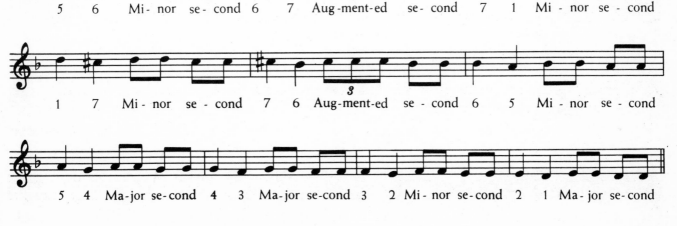

VOCALISES ON MODAL, CHROMATIC, AND WHOLE-TONE SCALE FORMS

1. MODAL SCALES: "MAJOR" TYPE

2. MODAL SCALES: "MINOR" TYPE

3. CHROMATIC SCALE

4. WHOLE-TONE SCALE

Critical listening

The important element in listening critically to scale types is that of noting the characteristics which are peculiar to each individual scale. This section presents first the familiar major and minor scale forms, then the less familiar modal forms, then all of these in combination.

Before these drills are performed, the student should label the given scale as to type, observing its structure closely as he does so. Ths following abbreviations are recommended for labelling the various types:

Pure major (Ionian mode)	I
Pure minor (Aeolian mode)	A
Melodic minor	mm
Harmonic minor	hm
Dorian mode	D
Phrygian mode	P
Lydian mode	L
Mixolydian mode	M

As the scales are played, the student should rewrite on the worksheet any scales that are played differently and label the new scale.

As always, the checking process may be a valuable vocalization drill. If the scale played differs from that printed, a student may respond by naming and singing the scale played, then singing the printed scale to contrast the two. If a wrong answer is given, a second student may illustrate the error by singing the contrasting scale types.

The work sheets may be re-used by placing music paper alongside the original version, so that after the variants given on the following pages have been used, new variants may be invented until the skills of scale spelling and scale type recognition have been mastered.

The student's success depends as much on his work by himself, reviewing the comparisons by singing and playing, as it does on his work with others in the classroom or in practice sessions.

MAJOR AND MINOR SCALE FORMS

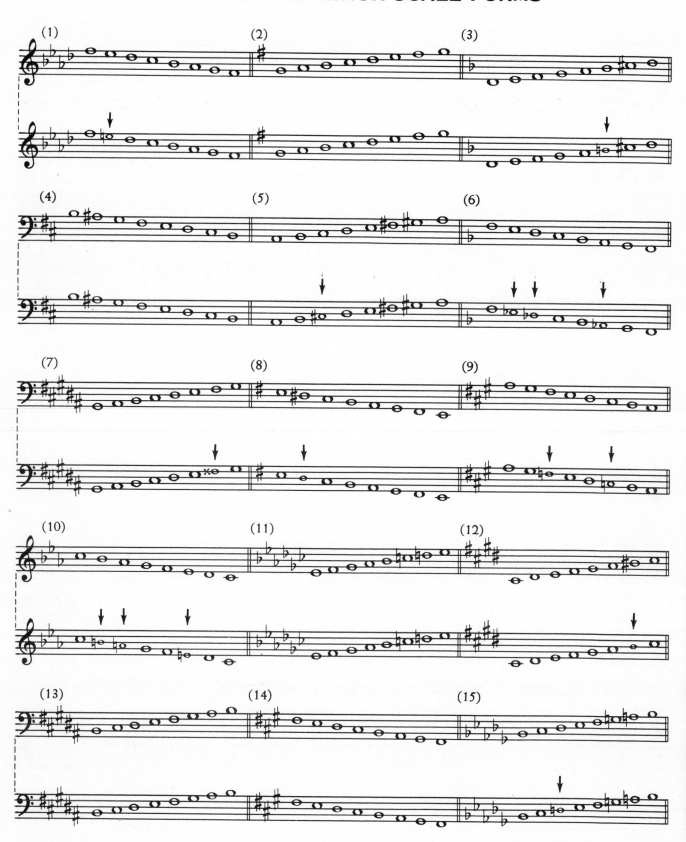

MODAL SCALE FORMS

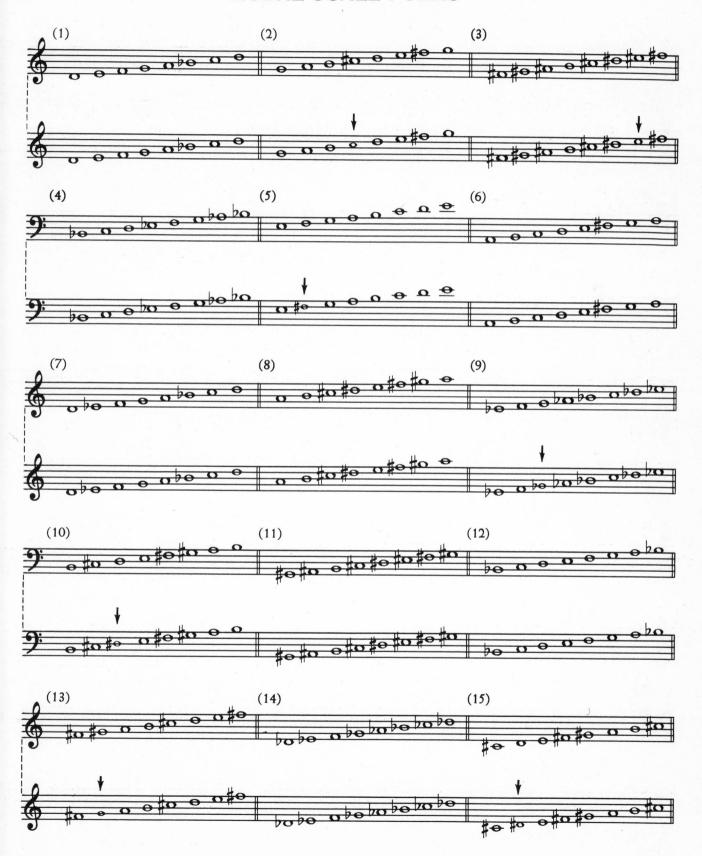

MAJOR, MINOR, AND MODAL SCALE FORMS

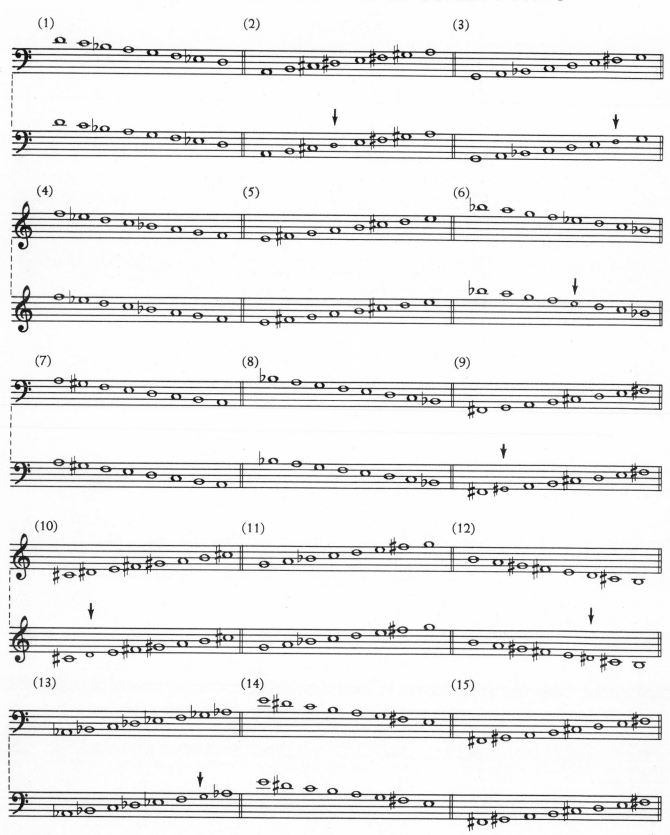

Dictation

Several groups of scales are provided here for convenience in dictation practice. The organization follows that of the preceding section. It will be easy for the instructor or student to devise further drills. When spelling practice as well as aural drill is desired, the keynote may be given and the scales written on the staff. For more rapid identification drill, the students may write down the type of scale heard, very quickly, by using the abbreviations listed in the *Critical listening* section of this chapter.

It is suggested that a further skill be cultivated by adding another problem to the identification drill on occasion: after playing the scale, repeat one tone, requiring the class or practice group to write the number of the scale degree isolated after the abbreviation for the scale type; as for example, A – 4 (pure minor scale, fourth degree repeated). The performer may circle lightly the note to be repeated at a particular time.

As always, speed of the drill and number of playings depend on the proficiency of the class or practice group.

MAJOR AND MINOR SCALE FORMS

MODAL SCALE FORMS

MAJOR, MINOR, AND MODAL SCALE FORMS

CHAPTER 3

INTERVALS

Basic drills

The facts concerning intervals are taught in a variety of ways; some textbooks base the teaching of intervals on the scale, others, on chords, and still others, on acoustical relationships. The vocalises presented here as *Basic drills* may be applied to any teaching procedure. Their purpose is to require the student to produce vocally the sounds of the various intervals while naming them, and later to learn to make fine vocal discrimination between intervals which are frequently confused in singing and in aural recognition.

The first set of drills, VOCALISES BASED ON MAJOR SCALE INTERVALS, deals with all intervals within the octave that are contained in the major scale. The VOCALISES BASED ON CHROMATIC SCALE INTERVALS involve all intervals within the octave that are contained in the chromatic scale. Exercises 4 through 7 focus attention on specific intervals and force the singer to depend on his knowledge of the intervallic sounds, without reference to any key or tone center. It is recommended that the vocalises in this last group be used as a preparatory drill to sight singing the music of composers such as Hindemith or Stravinsky wherein absolute knowledge of interval sounds is essential.

VOCALISES BASED ON MAJOR SCALE INTERVALS:
MAJOR, MINOR, AND PERFECT

1. ASCENDING INTERVALS

Per - fect   prime   Ma - jor   2nd   Ma - jor   3rd   Per - fect   4th

Per - fect   5th   Ma - jor   6th   Ma - jor   7th   Per - fect   8ve

2. DESCENDING INTERVALS

Per - fect   prime   Mi - nor   2nd   Mi - nor   3rd   Per - fect   4th

Per - fect   5th   Mi - nor   6th   Mi - nor   7th   Per - fect   8ve

3. ASCENDING AND DESCENDING INTERVALS CONTRASTED

Per - fect   prime   Per - fect   prime   Ma - jor   2nd   Mi - nor   2nd

Ma - jor   3rd   Mi - nor   3rd   Per - fect   4th   Per - fect   4th   Per - fect   5th   Per - fect   5th

Ma - jor   6th   Mi - nor   6th   Ma - jor   7th   Mi - nor   7th   Per - fect   8ve   Per - fect   8ve

4. INVERTED INTERVALS

Perfect   prime   Perfect   8 ve   Major   2nd   Minor   7th

Major   3rd   Minor   6th   Perfect   4th   Perfect   5th   Perfect   5th   Perfect   4th

Major   6th   Minor   3rd   Major   7th   Minor   2nd   Perfect   8ve   Perfect   prime

VOCALISES BASED ON CHROMATIC SCALE INTERVALS:
ALL INTERVAL TYPES

1. ASCENDING INTERVALS

Perfect prime Minor 2nd Major 2nd Minor 3rd Major 3rd Perfect 4th Augmented 4th

Diminished 5th Perfect 5th Minor 6th Major 6th Minor 7th Major 7th Perfect 8ve

2. DESCENDING INTERVALS

Perfect prime Minor 2nd Major 2nd Minor 3rd Major 3rd Perfect 4th Augmented 4th

Diminished 5th Perfect 5th Minor 6th Major 6th Minor 7th Major 7th Perfect 8ve

3. ASCENDING AND DESCENDING INTERVALS CONTRASTED

Minor 2nd Minor 2nd Major 2nd Major 2nd Minor 3rd

Minor 3rd Major 3rd Major 3rd Perfect 4th Perfect 4th Augmented 4th

Augmented 4th Diminished 5th Diminished 5th Perfect 5th Perfect 5th

Minor 6th Minor 6th Major 6th Major 6th Minor 7th

Minor 7th Major 7th Major 7th Perfect 8ve Perfect 8ve

4. EMPHASIZING MAJOR AND MINOR SECONDS

5. EMPHASIZING MAJOR AND MINOR THIRDS

6. EMPHASIZING PERFECT FOURTHS AND FIFTHS

7. EMPHASIZING AUGMENTED AND DIMINISHED INTERVALS

Selective listening

Interval *Selective listening* in a melodic context is neither a practical nor a musically effective type of drill. Instead, the problem of isolating the sound of each of the intervals within the octave is set up in blocks of ten unrelated intervals with the student placing check marks in the squares on the work sheet to indicate where he hears the interval in question.

It is suggested that the person giving the drill play each interval once only; the speed will be determined by the proficiency of the individual or group being drilled.

Although the problems are presented in terms of melodic intervals in order to drill both the ascending and descending forms of each interval, the same drills may be adapted to harmonic intervals by playing the tones simultaneously instead of consecutively. In this case the division into ascending and descending forms will be ignored.

It is hardly necessary to point out that the exercises are interchangeable to an extent, and one set of intervals may be used to serve more than one purpose; for example, the series of intervals provided for the perfect fifth may be used equally well for the perfect fourth, minor sixth, or tritone. When it is considered that any series of intervals may also be played backwards, the extent of possible variation becomes apparent.

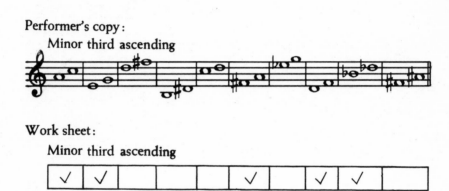

Performer's copy:

Minor third ascending

Work sheet:

Minor third ascending

MAJOR, MINOR AND PERFECT INTERVALS: ASCENDING AND DESCENDING

1. MAJOR SECOND (ASCENDING)

(DESCENDING)

2. MINOR SECOND (ASCENDING)

(DESCENDING)

3. MAJOR THIRD (ASCENDING)

(DESCENDING)

4. MINOR THIRD (ASCENDING)

(DESCENDING)

5. PERFECT FOURTH (ASCENDING)

(DESCENDING)

6. PERFECT FIFTH (ASCENDING)

(DESCENDING)

7. MAJOR SIXTH (**ASCENDING**)

(DESCENDING)

8. MINOR SIXTH (**ASCENDING**)

(DESCENDING)

9. MAJOR SEVENTH (ASCENDING)

TRITONE INTERVALS: ASCENDING AND DESCENDING

Critical listening

Carelessness in reading is nowhere more apparent than in the area of intervals. As the student proceeds with the drills in this section he may find himself focusing attention on the specific identity of intervals with an intensity never before experienced. It is easy to assume the nature of intervals encountered in simple melodic lines without subjecting them to close scrutiny, and careless reading habits are fostered; for this reason most students sight sing very badly when the music is written in an unfamiliar style and the specific identity of intervals cannot be predicted. The same weakness in intervallic recognition appears when students who do well in melodic dictation from sources such as Haydn are very inaccurate in attempting to take down a melody of Bartok or Schoenberg.

In doing this exercise, the student should first label the given interval in the blank provided. Then, as the intervals are played, the student should rewrite any that are played differently and relabel them.

The checking of exercises in class provides a fine opportunity for vocalization drill. The following routine is suggested:

1. The instructor plays the interval as it was played in the drill.

2. A student sings the interval back, first on *la* or *loo*, then by name (Ma-jor sixth), and finally by the names of the notes.

3. If the interval is played as it was written the student may say, "It is correct." If it is different from the written version he says, "It should have been —" then repeats the singing process, intoning, naming, and spelling the original interval. If he is in error, another student may make the correction by singing.

The unlimited possibilities for varying the errors to increase practice material are so obvious that no demonstration is necessary. The only limitation is in keeping the error within the realm of probability, as for example confusing a perfect fourth with a perfect fifth or a major sixth with a minor sixth. The exercises on page 85 include all types of intervals but place stress on augmented and diminished spellings.

The student is reminded of the importance of a review-comparison of his completed interval *Critical listening* exercises. The most effective method is to play the tone which was unchanged, sing the interval, then test by playing on the instrument. Special attention should always be given to intervals heard incorrectly in taking the drill.

MAJOR, MINOR, PERFECT, AND TRITONE INTERVALS

1. SIMPLE MELODIC INTERVALS

(First tone unchanged)

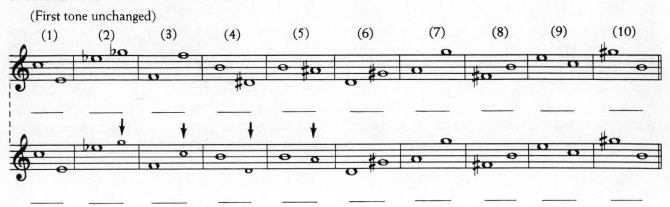

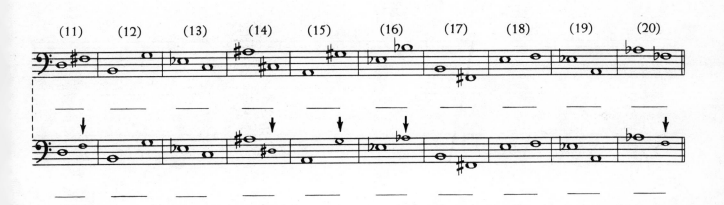

2. SIMPLE AND COMPOUND MELODIC INTERVALS

(First tone unchanged)

3. SIMPLE HARMONIC INTERVALS

(Lower tone unchanged)

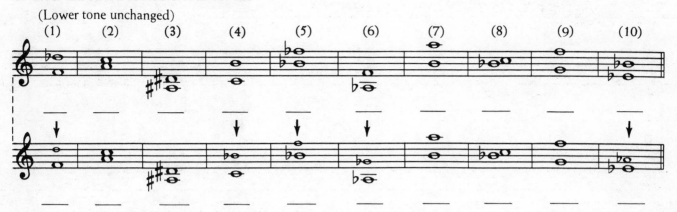

(Upper tone unchanged)

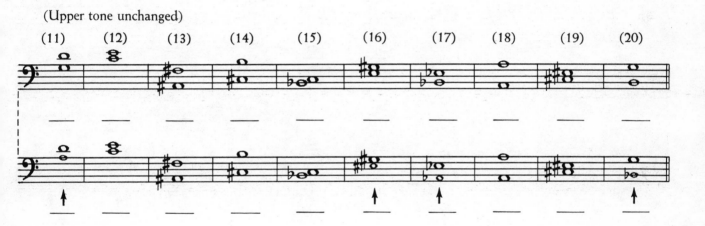

(Lower tone unchanged)

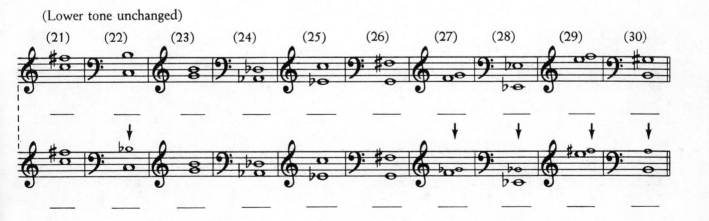

4. SIMPLE AND COMPOUND HARMONIC INTERVALS

(Lower tone unchanged)

(Upper tone unchanged)

(Upper tone unchanged)

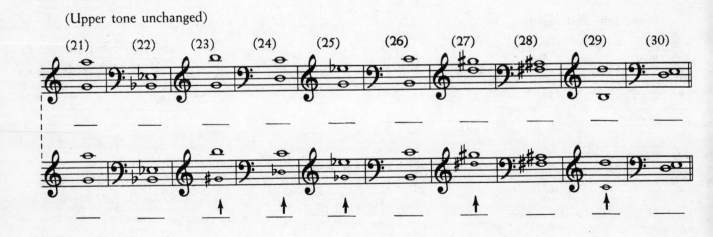

AUGMENTED AND DIMINISHED INTERVALS

1. SIMPLE AND COMPOUND MELODIC INTERVALS

(First tone unchanged)

(First tone unchanged)

2. SIMPLE AND COMPOUND HARMONIC INTERVALS

(Lower tone unchanged)

(Upper tone unchanged)

Dictation

As in the case of scales, two techniques may be used in dictating intervals. Sometimes the instructor will want his students to concentrate on rapid identification of interval types and record their results with shorthand symbols (P5, M6, etc.). At other times recognition drill may be coupled with spelling and notation drill, the instructor announcing the name of the first tone, lower tone, or upper tone, and requiring students to spell the intervals or write them on the staff.

Some of the drills provided involve rapid shifts from high to low octave registers. If this is to be a notation drill, the instructor may tell the octave register along with the pitch name of the first tone, or may make aural identification of octave register an additional dictation problem.

Since discrimination between the augmented fourth and the diminished fifth is not possible outside a tonal context, this interval sound may be identified simply as *Tritone* and the abbreviation TT may be used to indicate where it was heard. Obviously enharmonic equivalents of any interval spelling are acceptable.

MAJOR, MINOR, AND PERFECT INTERVALS

1. SIMPLE MELODIC INTERVALS

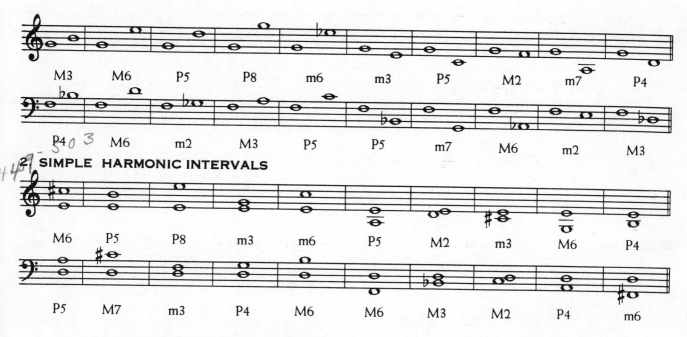

2. SIMPLE HARMONIC INTERVALS

MAJOR, MINOR, PERFECT, AND TRITONE INTERVALS

1. SIMPLE MELODIC INTERVALS

2. SIMPLE AND COMPOUND MELODIC INTERVALS

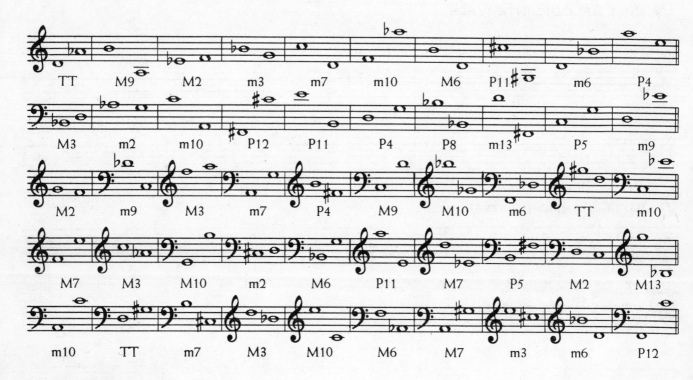

3. SIMPLE HARMONIC INTERVALS

4. SIMPLE AND COMPOUND HARMONIC INTERVALS

CHAPTER 4

Melody

Basic drills

Chapter 1 provided drill on rhythm without pitch; the present chapter begins with *Basic drills* on pitch without rhythm in the form of short melodic fragments for dictation. These are of two types: Melodic recognition drills and Melodic memory drills.

In the first group of Melodic recognition drills, each of the fragments is constructed so as to be clearly related to a single major or minor key. In the first part of this group, the key is identified on the student's work sheet and the first tone must be deduced; the performer may establish the key before playing these fragments. In the second part the first tone is given but the key must be determined by ear; here there must be no preliminary key establishment.

In the last group of Melodic recognition drills, the fragments are not derived from any familiar tonal association, and the student is dependent upon his hearing of absolute intervals. A review of the Vocalises based on chromatic scale intervals (Chapter 3, pages 69-72) is recommended at this time. With no key signature, spelling becomes more arbitrary, and the students' results may sometimes contain enharmonic equivalents of the original version. For the most part, however, the accepted practice of sharping notes that lead upward and flatting notes that lead downward will limit this tendency.

It will be noted that the first *Critical listening* drills in this chapter (pages 96-100) parallel the two types of melodic fragments described above. Often the dictation skill will improve if a *Critical listening* drill of similar nature precedes it.

The second set of *Basic drills*, entitled Melodic memory drills, is designed to help the student acquire speed in memorization of melodic patterns and translation of these patterns into notation.

Here, as in *Selective listening*, it is essential to move forward across prepared measures as the music moves ahead in time.

The following procedure is recommended for the MELODIC MEMORY DRILLS. The performer tells the class or practice group the meter signature, the number of measures, and the notation of the unvarying rhythmic pattern. (Rhythmic recognition is not sought here, merely rapid rhythmic notation in a drill aimed at the cultivation of speed.) When the measures have been barred off, the performer establishes the key, has the class sing the scale with letter names or solfege syllables, establishes the tempo, then plays the first one- or two-measure pattern (indicated by a bracket above the line). He waits for that many beats to elapse, then repeats the first pattern and adds the second. After waiting for the number of beats in the pattern he then repeats two and adds pattern three, and proceeds in this fashion until the entire exercise is dictated. Students must react and write very rapidly under these circumstances, and it may be necessary, at the outset, to take a relatively slow tempo or to double the time between playings. Details of rhythmic notation may be omitted during very rapid dictation.

Reference has been made to the improvement in music writing technique which results from the firmer grasp of the time-space relationship provided by *Selective listening*, and from the control of drawing and placement of symbols provided by *Critical listening*. The MELODIC MEMORY DRILLS attack another important problem in musical notation — that of achieving speed without loss of accuracy. In much practical dictation, it is necessary to sketch what is being heard in a sort of shorthand notation; the MELODIC MEMORY DRILLS provide a means for cultivating this skill. Special emphasis must be placed on clear spacing of rhythmic groupings and on careful distinction between noteheads on lines and those in spaces on the staff. Noteheads may be sketched in rapidly but clearly by using short horizontal dashes in spaces and diagonal dashes on the lines; if these are accurately grouped according to rhythmic placement the addition of stems, beams, flags, rests, ties, or dots may be accomplished very rapidly.

MELODIC RECOGNITION DRILLS

1. FRAGMENTS RELATED TO FAMILIAR SCALE FORMS

(Key given; identify scale degrees)

(First tone given; identify key and remaining tones and add key signature)

2. FRAGMENTS NOT RELATED TO FAMILIAR SCALE FORMS

(First tone given; identify remaining tones)

MELODIC MEMORY DRILLS

Critical listening

Melodic *Critical listening* with rhythmic errors only is found in Chapter 1; the drill that follows involves melodic fragments with pitch errors and melodies with errors in pitch and rhythm.

As in the rhythmic *Critical listening*, the student, on the first hearing, will note where what he hears differs from what he sees and, on later hearings, will write only that which is different in the corresponding blank measures below.

At the conclusion of the checking process (which should be, as always, a singing process), singing the melody in its original form is a good drill in accurate reading, since up to that point only the altered version has been heard.

Not only may the same exercises be re-used with new contrived errors, but new versions may be created inadvertently by performers who through carelessness or lack of skill are inaccurate in reading. It is of the utmost importance that the critical faculty being cultivated in the students be welcomed at all of its manifestations whether or not the errors were planned.

It is of increasing importance that the student, in reviewing his completed exercises, study the errors made, observe their nature, and note the probable cause for the various types in actual reading experience. If he lacks keyboard facility to play the more difficult melodies at a reasonable tempo he may sing them or play them on a wind or string instrument, making any necessary change of octave.

EXERCISES WITH PITCH ERRORS

1. FRAGMENTS RELATED TO FAMILIAR SCALE FORMS

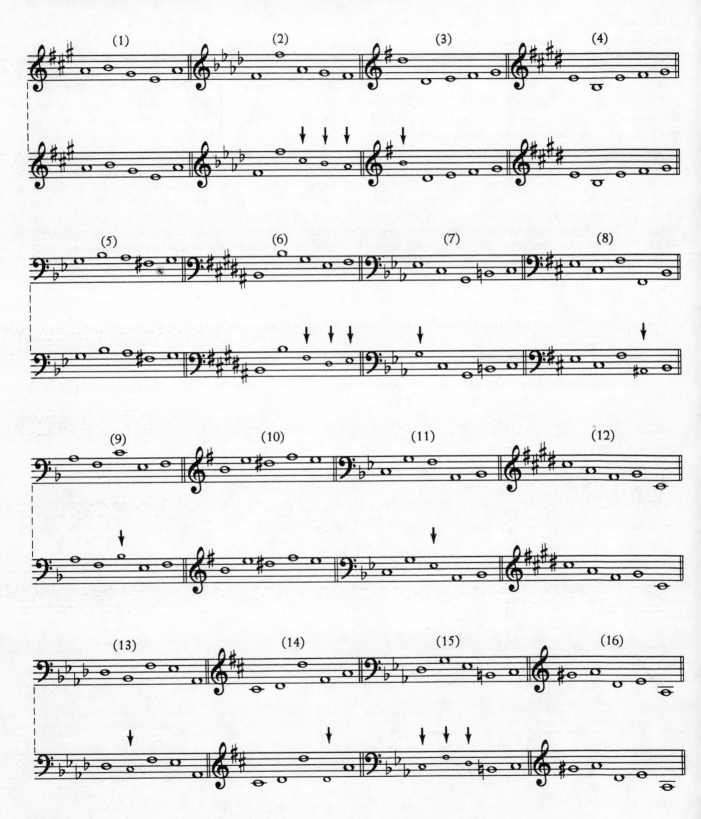

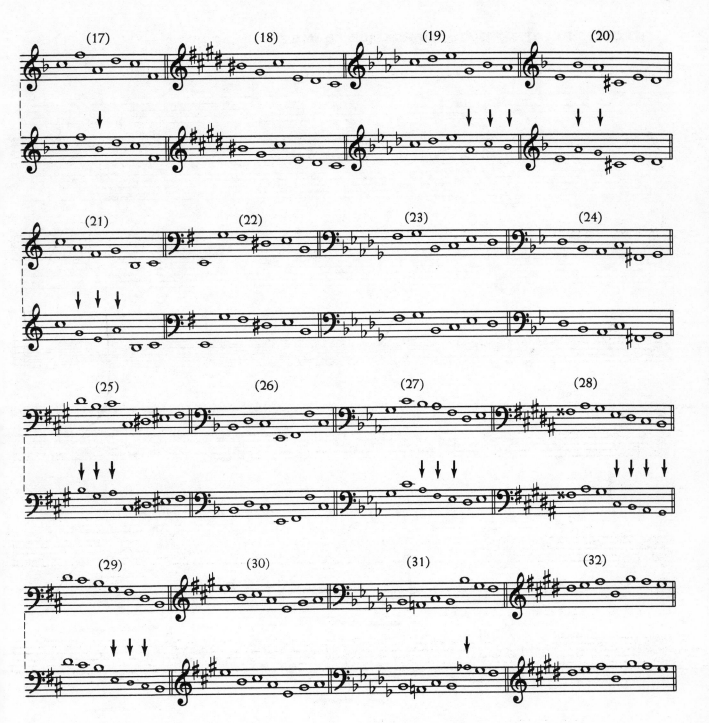

2. MELODIES RELATED TO FAMILIAR SCALE FORMS

(1)

(2)

(3)

(4)

(5)

(6)

(7)

3. FRAGMENTS NOT RELATED TO FAMILIAR SCALE FORMS

EXERCISES WITH PITCH AND RHYTHM ERRORS

1. MELODIES RELATED TO FAMILIAR SCALE FORMS

(4)

(5)

(6)

(7)

(8)

(9)

(10)

2. MODAL MELODIES

(1)

(2)

(3)

(4)

(5)

(6)

(7)

Dictation

The first melodic *Dictation* is given in the form of short themes, some of which will be familiar to the student. These themes are grouped according to their starting intervals; the student taking dictation is to be told only the first two tones, so that he must determine the key.

Melodic dictation drill of this type is an important part of the ear-training process. The student should not become dependent on hearing a preliminary establishment of key center; this is an unreal situation in terms of what happens in practical experience when he wishes to take down what he hears in a musical performance. Giving the identity of the first interval is close to actual experience in which the student has merely to *identify* the opening interval and (unless he has pitch recognition) to choose a reasonable pitch level at which to record it; he will then proceed in the manner being outlined here.

In order to locate key center, he must direct his attention first to the shape of the melody, noting which of its tones receive emphasis. He must have a fairly good impression of the melody as a whole before he assigns scale degree numbers to the two given tones. (The excerpts have been chosen so as to provide variety in the scale step identity of the given tones.) In a few cases, the quoted excerpts may be heard in terms of two possible key centers and correctly recorded in relation to either.

Grouping together several themes which share a common starting interval has the further advantage of bringing to the student's attention similarities and difference in the practice of composers in the evolution of a theme. The awareness thus achieved will provide insight which, in turn, will lead to quicker aural recognition of characteristic melodic treatment. As he proceeds in taking down a dictated theme, the student will notice such things as repetition, inversion, enlarging, or diminishing of the opening interval or of a motive of which it is a part. Performance of the themes must be clear and accurate to permit such listening.

With full-scale melodic dictation such as that found in the lists which follow we arrive at a point where the ear-training process can take place under conditions of actual performance. The melodies may be heard from the phonograph or the tape recorder; if they are performed by the instructor or a student on piano or another instrument or by singing, care must be taken that tempo and phrasing are correctly performed.

Whether longer melodic excerpts shall be dictated by phrases, or heard only in their entirety, will depend on the student's proficiency. It will be observed, however, that the skill achieved in *Selective listening* will enable him to keep his bearings in order to hear the melody not as a series of tones but as an aesthetic whole in which he is aware first of opening motive, cadence points, climax, and other significant structural elements. Generally the student's notation of a melody heard should grow "in patches", and the elements notated first should be the elements which contribute most to the aesthetic shape of the melody. In order for this process to occur it is necessary to perform the melody in its entirety.

LIST OF DICTATION FROM LITERATURE

Key to Rhythmic Characteristics

R1 Simple beat with division only
R2 Simple beat with easy subdivision
R3 Simple beat with more difficult subdivision
R4 Simple beat with problems involving rests, ties, or syncopation
R5 Simple beat with problems involving introduction of triplets and/or sextuplets
R6 Compound beat with division only
R7 Compound beat with easy subdivision
R8 Compound beat with more difficult subdivision
R9 Compound beat with problems involving rests, ties, or syncopation

1. Major or minor key, no modulation
   A. Largely stepwise melody with a few easy skips:
      (1) Beethoven: Symphony No. 9, fourth movement, mm. 99-107 (R1)
      (2) Beethoven: Symphony No. 8, first movement, mm. 1-12 (R2)
      (3) Brahms: Song: "Sandmännchen" (R1)
   B. Largely stepwise melody with more difficult skips:
      (1) Beethoven: Sonata in F major for violin and piano, Op. 24, first movement, mm. 1-10 (R2)
      (2) Mahler: *Lieder Eines Fahrenden Gesellen*, "Ging heut' morgen über's Feld," mm. 1-24 (R4)
   C. Fairly disjunct melody with easy intervals:
      (1) Bach: Well-tempered Clavier, Book I, Prelude in E major, mm. 1-3 (R6)
      (2) Bizet: *L'Arlésienne*, Suite No. 1, "Carillon," mm. 5-41 (involves much repetition) (R5)
      (3) Prokofieff: *Peter and the Wolf*, "The Cat," (R1)
      (4) Haydn: *The Creation*, No. 3, "Now Vanish Before the Holy Beams," mm. 54-67 (R1)
   D. Fairly disjunct melody with more difficult intervals:
      (1) Haydn: *The Creation*, No. 7, "Rolling in Foaming Billows," mm. 13-26 (R1)
      (2) Brahms: Symphony No. 1, fourth movement, mm. 132-139 (first oboe) (R5)
      (3) Brahms: Symphony No. 2, first movement, mm. 127-134 (R2)
   E. Largely disjunct melody with easy intervals:
      (1) Dvorak: Symphony No. 5, first movement, first theme, mm. 24-31 (R4)
      (2) Beethoven: Symphony No. 6, fifth movement, mm. 9-16 (R6)
      (3) Handel: *Messiah*, "The Trumpet Shall Sound," mm. 29-40 (R1)
      (4) Haydn: *The Creation*, No. 29, "Of Stars the Fairest," mm. 7-24 (R2)
   F. Largely disjunct melody with more difficult intervals:
      (1) Bach: Well-tempered Clavier, Book I, Fugue in C Sharp Major, mm. 1-3 (R2)
      (2) Schumann: Quintet in E♭ major for piano and strings, Op. 44, first movement, mm. 1-9 (R1)
      (3) Brahms: Symphony No. 2, first movement, mm. 110-127 (R4)
      (4) Richard Strauss: *Ein Heldenleben*, Op. 40 (orchestra) mm. 1-9 (R4)

2. Major or minor key with modulation
   A. Largely stepwise melody with a few easy skips:
      (1) Beethoven: Symphony No. 1, fourth movement, m. 6-22 (R2)
      (2) Verdi: *Requiem*, Agnus Dei, mm. 1-13 and 27-39 (R5)
      (3) Bach: *St. John Passion*, No. 13, "I Follow Thee Also," mm. 17-40 (R2)
      (4) Brahms: Symphony No. 1, third movement, mm. 1-18 (R2)
   B. Largely stepwise melody with more difficult skips:
      (1) Bach: *Magnificat*, No. 3, "Quia respexit," mm. 6-14 (R3)
      (2) Bach: *Magnificat*, No. 8, "Deposuit," mm. 15-28 (R2)
      (3) Mendelssohn: *Elijah*, No. 26, "It is Enough," mm. 10-30 (R1)
   C. Fairly disjunct melody with easy intervals:
      (1) Beethoven: Symphony No. 5, second movement, mm. 1-8 (R2)
      (2) Beethoven: Symphony No. 7, third movement, mm. 1-24 (R6)
      (3) Schubert: Octet in F major, Op. 166, fourth movement, mm. 1-24 (R4)

D. Fairly disjunct melody with more difficult intervals:
  (1) Bach: Well-tempered Clavier, Book I, Fugue in E minor, mm. 1-3 (R2)
  (2) Brahms: "Wir Wandelten," Op. 96, No. 2 (R1)
  (3) Haydn: *The Creation*, No. 27a, "On Thee Each Living Soul Awaits," mm. 36-54 (R1)
E. Largely disjunct melody with easy intervals:
  (1) Mendelssohn: Violin Concerto in E minor, Op. 64, Andante, mm. 537-554 (violin solo) (R7)
  (2) Beethoven: Piano Sonata in F major, Op. 10, No. 2, second movement, first theme, mm. 1-8 (R1)
  (3) Schumann: "Auftrage," Op. 77, No. 5, mm. 1-12 (R3)
F. Largely disjunct melody with more difficult intervals:
  (1) Brahms: Symphony No. 4, first movement, first theme, mm. 1-19 (R2)
  (2) Brahms: "Feldeinsamkeit," Op. 86, No. 2 (R2)
  (3) Shostakovich: Symphony No. 5, first movement, second theme, mm. 51-74 (R1)
  (4) Prokofieff: *Peter and the Wolf*, "Peter," (R2)

3. Modal melodies
  A. Largely stepwise melody with a few easy skips:
    (1) Bartok: Fifteen Hungarian Peasant Songs (piano), No. 2, Dorian (R7 & 9)
    (2) Dvorak: Symphony No. 5, first movement, second theme, mm. 91-94, Aeolian (R2)
    (3) Chopin: Mazurka, Op. 41, No. 1, mm. 1-8, Phrygian (R2)
    (4) Bartok: *Mikrokosmos* (piano), No. 40, Mixolydian (R1)
    (5) Bartok: Rumanian Folk Dances (piano), No. 2, Dorian (R3)
    (6) Bartok: Fifteen Hungarian Peasant Songs, Nos. 9 & 10, Dorian (R1)
    (7) Bartok: Rumanian Folk Dances No. 6, mm. 1-8, Lydian (R2)
  B. Largely stepwise melody with more difficult skips:
    (1) Vaughan Williams: "Withers' Rocking Hymn," Oxford Book of Carols, No. 185, Aeolian (R1)
    (2) Delius: *Brigg Fair* (orchestra), theme (as stated by oboe) Dorian (R8)
    (3) Mussorgsky: *Pictures at an Exhibition*, "The Old Castle," mm. 8-28, Aeolian-Phrygian (R7)
  C. Fairly disjunct melody with easy intervals:
    (1) Arr. Vaughan Williams: "A Virgin Most Pure," Oxford Book of Carols, Appendix No. 1, Dorian (R1)
    (2) Wayne Barlow: *The Winter's Past* (orchestra), Mixolydian, oboe solo (R5)
    (3) Dupré: Variations On a Noel (organ) theme, Dorian (R2)
    (4) Chopin: Mazurka, Op. 24, No. 2, mm. 21-28, Lydian (R5)
  D. Fairly disjunct melody with more difficult intervals:
    (1) Prokofieff: Piano Concerto No. 3, Op. 26, third movement, first theme, Aeolian, mm. 1-9 (R1 but effect of changing meter)
    (2) Kodály: *Háry János* Suite, Op. 15, "The Battle and Defeat of Napoleon," mm. 5-12 (more if desired) Dorian (R3)
4. Melodies based on familiar scale forms but involving extensive chromaticism
  A. Largely stepwise melody with a few easy skips:
    (1) Franck: Symphony in D minor, second movement, mm. 17-48 (involves much repetition) (R1)

(2) Prokofieff: *Peter and the Wolf,* "The Bird" (R5)

(3) Tschaikovsky: Symphony No. 4, first movement, first theme, mm. 28-35 (R8)

(4) Bartok: Rumanian Folk Dances (piano), No. 4 (R4)

B. Largely stepwise melody with more difficult skips:

(1) Prokofieff: *Peter and the Wolf,* "March of the Hunters" (R5)

(2) Menotti: *The Medium,* beginning of Act II, Monica, solo "Up in the Sky" (R6)

(3) Prokofieff: *Peter and the Wolf,* "The Grandfather," (R5)

C. Fairly disjunct melody with easy intervals:

(1) Wagner: *Tannhäuser,* Overture, first theme, part 2, mm. 17-32 (R2)

(2) Prokofieff: *Peter and the Wolf,* "The Duck" (R1)

D. Fairly disjunct melody with more difficult intervals:

(1) Shostakovich: Symphony No. 1, first movement, first theme, mm. 58-65 (R5)

(2) Shostakovich: Symphony No. 5, second movement, second theme, mm. 45-55 (R2)

(3) Richard Strauss: *Don Juan,* Op. 20 (orchestra), mm. 9-17 (R2)

E. Largely disjunct melody with easy intervals :

(1) Prokofieff: *Classical Symphony,* Gavotte, mm. 1-12 (R1)

(2) Stravinsky: *Firebird Suite,* Berceuse, mm. 3-16 (R5)

F. Largely disjunct melody with more difficult intervals:

(1) Ravel: *Le Tombeau de Couperin,* "Forlane," mm. 1-5 (R7)

(2) Hindemith: *Symphonic Metamorphosis of Themes by C. M. von Weber,* "Turandot," mm. 2-17 (R5)

(3) Kodály: *Háry János* Suite Op. 15, "The Battle and Defeat of Napoleon," mm. 103-112 (R1)

5. Melodies not based on familiar scale forms

A. Largely stepwise melody with a few easy skips:

(1) Mussorgsky: *Pictures at an Exhibition,* "Tuileries," mm. 1-11 (R2)

(2) Honegger: *King David,* No. 18, "Song of the Handmaid" (R1)

(3) Honegger: *King David,* No. 25, "In My Distress" (R5)

B. Largely stepwise melody with more difficult skips

(1) Hindemith: Symphony *Mathis der Mahler,* first movement, second theme, mm. 39-54 (R4)

(2) Shostakovich: Symphony No. 5, first movement, first theme, section two, mm. 6-12 (R3)

C. Fairly disjunct melody:

(1) Menotti: *Amahl and the Night Visitors,* Entrance of the Kings (as many measures as desired) (R2)

(2) Hindemith: *Ludus Tonalis,* third fugue, mm. 1-7 (R1)

D. Largely disjunct melody:

(1) Hindemith: *Ludus Tonalis,* second Interludium "Pastorale" (R8)

(2) Debussy: *Nocturnes* (orchestra) "Fetes," fourth theme, (muted trumpets), mm. 116-131 (R5)

(3) Schoenberg: String Quartet, Op. 37, third movement, mm. 1-5 (R5) (statement of 12-tone row)

(4) Hindemith: *Ludus Tonalis,* fifth fugue, mm. 1-8 (R6)

MELODIES GROUPED BY STARTING INTERVAL

1. MINOR SECOND (ASCENDING AND DESCENDING)

Bach: Brandenburg Concerto No. 3, first movement

Presto

Haydn: String Quartet in G major, Op. 77 No. 1, last movement

Bizet: *Carmen*, "Habanera"

Hindemith: Third Piano Sonata, third movement

Mässig schnell

2. MAJOR SECOND (ASCENDING AND DESCENDING)

Andante

Mozart: *The Marriage of Figaro*, Act III, "Dove sono"

Allegro

Beethoven: Symphony No. 5 in C minor, fourth movement

Allegro energico

Brahms: Ballade Op. 118 No. 3

Allegro non troppo

Tschaikovsky: Symphony No. 6 in B minor ("Pathetic") first movement

Moderato assai, quasi andante

Tschaikovsky: Symphony No. 4 in F minor, first movement

Andante grazioso

Mozart: *Don Giovanni*, Act I, "Batti, batti, o bel Masetto"

Allegro moderato

Tschaikovsky: Symphony No. 5 in E minor, third movement

Allegro

Brahms: Double Concerto for Violin and Violoncello in A minor, Op. 102 first movement

Allegro

Schubert: Piano Sonata in A major, Op. 120, third movement

Allegro moderato

Tschaikovsky: *The Seasons*, Op. 37A, "Troika"

Animé et très décidé

Debussy: String Quartet, Op. 10, first movement

Permission for reprint granted by Durand et Cie., Paris, France.
Copyright owners: Elkan-Vogel Co., Phila., Pa., agents.

3. MINOR THIRD (ASCENDING AND DESCENDING)

Handel: *Water Music,* "Air"

Bach: English Suite No. 3, "Gavotte"

Mendelssohn: Violin Concerto in E minor, Op. 64, third movement

Allegro molto vivace

Vivace

Smetana: *The Bartered Bride,* Act III, "Dance of the Comedians"

Allegro

Wagner: *Tannhäuser,* Act III, "Bacchanale"

Lent

Ravel: *Ma Mère L'Oye,* "Pavane de la Belle au bois dormant"

4. MAJOR THIRD(ASCENDING AND DESCENDING)

5. PERECT FOURTH(ASCENDING AND DESCENDING)

Largo cantabile — Haydn: Symphony No. 93 in D major, second movement

Andantino simplice — Tschaikowsky: Piano Concerto No. 1 in B♭ minor, Op. 23, second movement

Tempo di Valse — Tschaikowsky: *Nutcracker Suite*, "Waltz of the Flowers"

6. PERFECT FIFTH(ASCENDING AND DESCENDING)

Bach: Passacaglia in C minor for organ

Moderato con anima — Tschaikowsky: Symphony No. 5 in E minor, second movement

Andantino — Borodin: *Prince Igor*, "Polovetsian Dances"

Allegro molto — Beethoven: Symphony No. 3 in E♭ major ("Eroica") fourth movement

Larghetto — Beethoven: Symphony No. 2 in D major, second movement

Moderato — Tschaikowsky: *The Swan Lake*, Op. 20, First Scene

Innig — Schumann: *Liederalbum für die Jugend*, Op. 79 No. 23, "Er ist's"

Allegro — Handel: Concerto No. 3 in G minor for oboe and orchestra, second movement

Vivace — Liszt: Hungarian Rhapsody No. 2

Adagio — Mozart: Quartet in F major for oboe and strings, K. 370, second movement

7. MINOR SIXTH (ASCENDING AND DESCENDING)

Allegro — Brahms: Trio in A minor for piano, violin and clarinet (or viola), Op. 114, fourth movement

Allegro non troppo — Brahms: String Quartet in A minor, Op. 51, No. 2, first movement

Allegretto — Beethoven: Piano Sonata in D minor, Op. 31, No. 2, third movement

Allegro non troppo — Mendelssohn: *Song Without Words*, Op. 38, No. 2, "Lost Happiness"

Presto con brio — Mendelssohn: String Quartet in D major, Op. 44, No. 1, fourth movement

Mouvement de Valse viennoise — Ravel: *La Valse*

Permission for reprint granted by Durand et Cie., Paris, France.
Copyright owners: Elkan-Vogel Co., Phila., Pa., agents.

Allegro moderato — Mendelssohn: *Elijah*, Op. 70, "Blessed Are the Men"

Ziemlich langsam — Schubert: *Erlafsee*, Op. 8, No. 3

Rameau: "Les Sauvages"

Andante maestoso — Rossini: *Stabat Mater*, "Inflammatus"

Con affetto — Schumann: *Carnaval*, Op. 9 "Estrella"

8. MAJOR SIXTH (ASCENDING AND DESCENDING)

Allegretto — Verdi: *La Traviata*, Act III, "Libiamo ne' lieti calici"

Molto sostenuto e maestoso — Wagner: *Rienzi*, Overture

Bach: Partita No. 3 for violin unaccompanied, "Gavotte en Rondeau"

Wagner: *Die Miestersinger von Nürnberg*, Act I Scene II, Chorus of Apprentices

Chopin: Nocturne in Eb, Op. 9, No. 2

Andante

Copland: *El Salon Mexico*

Copyright 1949 by Hawkes and Son (London) Ltd.
Reprinted by permission of Boosey and Hawkes, Inc.

Allegro vivace

Bach: Well-tempered Clavier, Book I, prelude in C minor

Traurig, doch gelassen

Mozart: "Sei du Mein Trost," K. 391

Allegro Moderato

Handel: *Judas Maccabeus*, "Fall'n Is the Foe"

Vivace

Chopin: Mazurka in B major, Op. 63, No. 1

Geschwind und kräftig

Schubert "Heliopolis"

Sight singing

Sight singing, like *Dictation*, involves a fusion of all the skills being cultivated as part of the ear-training program. This interplay of skills will be illustrated here in terms of one of the melodies listed as recommended *Sight singing* in the present chapter, but reference will be made to contrapuntal and harmonic aspects of the melody in relation to its accompaniment, so that the discussion also relates to the *Sight singing* practiced in connection with the remaining chapters of the book.

The following excerpt is taken from the soprano solo which opens the Libera Me section of the Verdi *Requiem*.

The rhythmic skills of accurate reading, cultivated in *Critical listening,* and accurate performance, cultivated in rhythmic ensemble, are called forth in sight singing this melody, especially in precise observation of the rests in measures 1, 13, 20, and 21, in recognizing and performing the rhythmic patterns in measures 4 and 5, and in giving full value to the long notes in measures 11, 12, 22, and 23. The various rhythmic skills in combination will insure maintenance of a steady tempo.

Careful intonation of the chromatic scale in scale vocalization will contribute to the performance of measures 2, 3, 14, and 15, and the quick visual recognition of intervals, fostered by *Critical listening,* will facilitate the singing of measures 6 and 18, as will the vocal command of intervals achieved through vocalises.

Rapid comprehension of the melodic design, cultivated in the present chapter, will contribute to recognizing the relationship between measures 1 and 2 and measures 13 and 14, as well as the dramatic shape of measures 18 and 19. In a larger sense, melodic understanding will lead to a quick grasp of phrasing and direction.

Up to this point we have spoken in terms of the melody as standing apart from its accompaniment. Much benefit is to be gained from sight singing a melody apart from its contrapuntal and harmonic associations or from sight singing melodies which have been written to stand alone. Equally important, however, is practice in sight singing which involves adapting one's own part to another or to an ensemble, not only from a technical standpoint but in order to gain insight into the music itself.

The skills demanded for the latter type of sight singing will be cultivated in the chapters which follow. Turning again to the example from the Verdi *Requiem,* we find that intervallic problems such as the chromatic scale in measures 2 and 3 and the leaps in measure 6 present a different aspect when it is necessary to hear them as counterpoint to another strong line such as the cello line in the measures cited. Finally, comprehension and performance of the melody is greatly enhanced by awareness of the function of certain of the tones in the harmonic texture. The most noteworthy illustration of this is the note C at the beginning of measure 8. When the melody is seen by itself the C appears to be a point of repose, suggesting arrival at the tonic chord, with the following B-natural as an active tone, tending to resolve to C; addition of the accompaniment reveals that the C is seventh of a secondary dominant structure and significant chiefly for its tendency to resolve to the B. Performance of measure 18 becomes easier when the second half of the measure is heard against the Neapolitan sixth sonority, and knowledge of the accompaniment makes the importance and impressiveness of the final E-natural much more apparent.

The brief lists of *Sight singing* material which appear in the remaining chapters are chosen from material likely to be available in quantity in most school libraries and are intended only as illustrations of the type of material recommended. Students as well as instructors should explore the resources of the library with special attention to less standard repertory and to pre-Baroque and contemporary music. In Chapters 6, 7, and 8 short excerpts for *Sight singing* have been provided in the text for the convenience of students and teacher.

LIST OF SIGHT SINGING FROM LITERATURE

1. Major or minor key, no modulation
   A. Largely stepwise melody with a few easy skips:
      (1) Purcell: *Dido and Aeneas,* No. 10, "Pursue Thy Conquest, Love"
   B. Largely stepwise melody with more difficult skips:
      (1) Haydn: *The Creation,* No. 29, "Ye Purling Fountains" (Eve's solo)
   C. Fairly disjunct melody with easy intervals:
      (1) Mendelssohn: *Elijah,* No. 81, "O Rest in the Lord," mm. 1-11
      (2) Haydn: *The Creation.* No. 16, "On Mighty Pens," first 14 measures of solo
   D. Fairly disjunct melody with more difficult intervals:
      (1) Verdi: *Requiem,* Libera Me, mm. 21-43

E. Largely disjunct melody with easy intervals:
  (1) Haydn: *The Creation*, No. 25, "In Native Worth," first 12 measures of solo
  (2) Haydn: *The Creation*, No. 31, "Graceful Consort" (Adam's opening solo)

2. Major or minor key with modulation
  A. Largely stepwise melody with a few easy skips:
    (1) Bach: *Magnificat*, No. 2, "Et Exultavit"
    (2) Honegger: *King David*, No. 3, "All Praise to Him"
  B. Largely stepwise melody with more difficult skips:
    (1) Bach: *St. Matthew Passion*, No. 61, "If My Tears Be Unavailing"
  C. Fairly disjunct melody with easy intervals:
    (1) Purcell: *Dido and Aeneas*, No. 26, "Haste, Haste to Town," mm. 1-11
    (2) Haydn: *The Creation*, No. 19, "Most Beautiful Appear"
  D. Fairly disjunct melody with more difficult intervals:
    (1) Bach: *St. Matthew Passion*, No. 51, "Bring Him Back Is All My Prayer"
    (2) Mendelssohn: *Elijah*, No. 8, "What Have I To Do With Thee?", mm. 6-64
  E. Largely disjunct melody:
    (1) Bach: *St. Matthew Passion*, No. 9, "O Blessed Saviour"
    (2) Bach: *St. Matthew Passion*, No. 75, "Make Thee Clean, My Heart, From Sin"

3. Modal melodies
  A. Largely stepwise melody:
    (1) Honegger: *King David*, No. 2, "The Song of David, the Shepherd"
    (2) arr. Geoffrey Shaw: "Spring Has Come," Oxford Book of Carols, No. 98
    (3) arr. Vaughan Williams: "The Seven Virgins," Oxford Book of Carols, No. 43
  B. Fairly disjunct melody:
    (1) Honegger: *King David*, No. 9, "Pity Me Lord," mm. 3-11
    (2) arr. Vaughan Williams: "The Carnal and the Crane," Oxford Book of Carols, No. 53

4. Melodies based on familiar scale forms but involving extensive chromaticism
  A. Largely stepwise melody:
    (1) Honegger: *King David*, No. 7, "O Had I Wings"
    (2) Honegger: *King David*, No. 9, "Pity Me, Lord," mm. 14-29
  B. Fairly disjunct melody:
    (1) Honegger: *King David*, No. 21, "O Shall I Raise Mine Eyes"
    (2) Mendelssohn: *Elijah*, No. 14, "Lord God of Abraham"
  C. Largely disjunct melody:
    (1) Mendelssohn: *Elijah*, No. 17, "Is Not His Word Like a Fire?"

CHAPTER 5

Two-voice counterpoint

No specific *Basic drills* are given in connection with two-voice counterpoint. A review of harmonic intervals in *Selective listening*, *Critical listening*, and *Dictation* in Chapter 3 is advisable. Other preparation will be conditioned by the point in the course of study at which two-voice counterpoint is introduced.

Critical listening

The *Critical listening* exercises in two-voice counterpoint are divided into three groups: SELECTIONS WITH PITCH ERRORS; SELECTIONS WITH RHYTHM ERRORS; and SELECTIONS WITH PITCH AND RHYTHM ERRORS. In the first section the earliest exercises exclude the problem of rhythm altogether.

It is very important that the student be conscious of the duality of the listening process, dividing his attention between the horizontal relationships within each of the lines and the vertical relationships existing between the two lines. As always, the impressions received most strongly will be recorded first. Careful attention to these principles in *Critical listening* drill will lay a foundation for greater efficiency in taking two-voice contrapuntal dictation.

Work sheets may be re-used by placing music paper alongside the original version. In inventing new variants the instructor or the students must take care to create plausible errors, such as changing a neighboring tone from a whole step to a half step, sequentially imitating a previous rhythmic pattern, or replacing a wide intervallic leap with a smaller one suggesting the same harmonic background. Valuable classroom discussion may stem from having a student prepare and conduct a *Critical listening* drill then calling on other students for critical judgment of the drills contrived.

Thoughtful review of finished exercises is an integral part of the drill. From this point onward the complexity of the material requires some keyboard facility, and a student with little piano training may need to review in company with another who is able to play the exercises accurately and at a reasonable tempo.

SELECTIONS WITH PITCH ERRORS

SELECTIONS WITH RHYTHM ERRORS

(3)

(4)

(5)

(6)

(7)

(8)

SELECTIONS WITH PITCH AND RHYTHM ERRORS

(1)

(2)

(3)

(4)

(5)

(6)

(7)

136 · T W O - V O I C E   C O U N T E R P O I N T

Dictation

Because of the necessity of following independent lines in two-voice counterpoint, dictation from recorded or live performances, with contrasts of instrumental or vocal timbre, is more effective than dictation from the piano. Nevertheless, much excellent two-voice material is written for piano solo and is available for use where only piano is provided.

The observations previously made concerning rhythmic and melodic dictation apply here as well. Insofar as possible the performance should be a thoroughly artistic one as regards tempo, dynamics, phrasing, etc. For this reason students in practice sessions are encouraged to play from fully edited publications whenever possible.

LIST OF DICTATION FROM LITERATURE

1. Piano Music
   (1) Mozart: Piano Sonata, No. 13 in B♭ major, K. 333, third movement, mm. 1-8 (brief entry of third voice may be omitted in dictation)
   (2) Bartok: *Mikrokosmos,* Volume I, Nos. 23, 24, 28, 32, 34; Volume III, Nos. 78, 79
   (3) D. Scarlatti: Sonata in F major, Longo No. 432, mm. 1-8
   (4) Haydn: Piano Sonata No. 14 (Peters), Menuetto, mm. 1-8.
   (5) Beethoven: Piano Sonata No. 8 in C minor, Op. 13, third movement, mm. 79-86
   (6) Bach: English Suite, No. 5, Passepied I (as many measures as desired)
   (7) Bach: French Suite, No. 2, Menuet (as many measures as desired)

2. Instrumental Duos
   (1) Bartok: Violin Duets, Nos. 4, 14 (mm. 1-20), 18 (mm. 1-9), and 37 (mm. 1-17)
   (2) Mozart: Duo in B flat for violin and viola, K. 424, Adagio, mm. 1-12
   (3) Mozart: Duo in B flat for violin and viola, K. 424, Andante, mm. 1-16 (double stops at cadence)
   (4) Beethoven: Duo No. 2 for clarinet and bassoon, Larghetto, mm. 1-16
   (5) Beethoven: Duo No. 3 for clarinet and bassoon, theme and variations
   (6) Beethoven: Duet No. 2 for violin and cello, Rondo, mm. 1-20
   (7) Haydn: String Quartet, Op. 77, No. 2, third movement, mm. 1-8 (violin and cello duet)
   (8) Haydn: String Quartet, Op. 33, No. 2, third movement, mm. 1-8 (viola and cello duet)

3. Vocal Duos
   (1) Menotti: *The Medium,* end of Act I, duet, Monica and Baba, "The Spools Unravel"
   (2) Haydn: *The Creation,* No. 27a, "On Thee Each Living Soul Awaits," mm. 5-22
   (3) Haydn: *The Creation,* No. 29, "By Thee With Bliss," mm. 5-23
   (4) Haydn: *The Creation,* No. 29 (later section), "Ye Valleys, Hills, and Shady Woods" (duet of Eve and Adam)

NOTE: Excellent two-voice dictation practice may be derived from the 371 chorales of J. S. Bach by playing the soprano and bass lines only. Often this will be a preliminary stage in the harmonic dictation of a chorale.

Sight singing

LIST OF SIGHT SINGING FROM LITERATURE

(1) Purcell: *Dido and Aeneas*, No. 19, "But, Ere We This Perform."

(2) Verdi: *Requiem*, Dies Irae, "Recordare Jesu pie," mm. 383-445 (or shorter section)

(3) Verdi: *Requiem*, Dies Irae, "Lacrymosa," mm. 625-641.

(4) Bach: *St. Matthew Passion*, No. 33, "Behold My Saviour Now Is Taken."

(5) Bach: *Magnificat*, No. 6, "Et Misericordia."

(6) Handel: *Messiah*, "Oh Death, Where Is Thy Sting."

(7) Honegger: *King David*, No. 8, "Song of the Prophets."

(8) Honegger: *King David*, No. 19, "Psalm of Penitence."

NOTE: Valuable two-voice singing practice may be had by singing the soprano and bass lines of virtually any of the 371 chorales of J. S. Bach.

CHAPTER 6

TRIADS

Basic drills

The *Basic drills* on triads include TRIAD VOCALISES (I) and (II), TRIAD TYPE IDENTIFICATION, and TRIAD-IN-KEY VOCALISES.

The TRIAD VOCALISES (I) lend themselves to a variety of treatments. They may be used in their original form to check the student's accuracy of vocal intonation and to permit him to compare the sound and intervallic content of the four types of triads; they may be sung with letter names or solfege syllables instead of numbers, using a variety of starting tones; the individual patterns may be called for at random so that the student is forced to think of the total intervallic content of the specific triad type instead of varying one element at a time as in the vocalises; and the patterns should be used as a silent testing device and as a vocal means of communication in oral response with the TRIAD TYPE IDENTIFICATION which follows. Finally the patterns are available to make the thinking process audible throughout the remainder of the course of study, as will be indicated in later sections.

The TRIAD VOCALISES (II) clarify the intervallic relationships produced when the chord degrees are placed in all possible relationships to one another. They are especially useful in *Dictation* and *Critical listening* when the function of the soprano or bass tone in the chord must be determined.

The TRIAD TYPE IDENTIFICATION may be used in several ways. Any of the drills may be used for rapid identification of type only, using the familiar abbreviations, M for Major, m for minor, A for Augmented, and d for diminished. In addition to triad type identification, drills 2, 3, and 4 may be used for identifying soprano position and inversion, if any. For these drills, it is recommended that the student set up three columns, labelled T (type), S (soprano position), and B (chord degree in the bass). For the triads in four-part harmony in root position, the first two columns only would be used, and the exercise would appear as follows:

T S
1. M   3   (Major triad with third in soprano)
2. d   5   (diminished triad with fifth in soprano)
etc.

For the triads in root position and inversions, it is advisable, at least at the outset, to play each chord twice, emphasizing the soprano slightly at one time and the bass slightly the other. Finally, as in the case of scales and intervals, this drill will be combined with spelling and notation, requiring the student to place the chord on the staff, having been told the identity of root, highest tone, or lowest tone. This technique will be improved by coupling it with the *Critical listening* drills on isolated triads to be found in this chapter.

The initial function of the TRIAD-IN-KEY VOCALISES is that of organizing the student's thinking as to the type of triad found on each degree of the major or harmonic minor scale, the identity of the other scale degrees involved in each triad, the spelling of the triad in a selected key, and, simultaneously, the correct vocal intonation of each triad. As soon as these vocalises are understood and can be performed with relative fluency they may be used as a means of vocal key establishment in preparing for drills involving harmonic progression.

TRIAD VOCALISES (I)

TRIAD VOCALISES (II)

A. Basic patterns on a single chord.
C. All patterns up from a single tone.

B. Basic patterns from a single tone.
D. All patterns down from a single tone.

1. MAJOR TRIADS

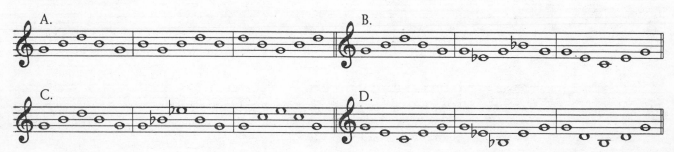

2. MINOR TRIADS

3. DIMINISHED TRIADS

4. AUGMENTED TRIADS

TRIAD TYPE IDENTIFICATION

1. TRIADS IN ROOT POSITION

2. TRIADS IN ROOT POSITION AND INVERSIONS

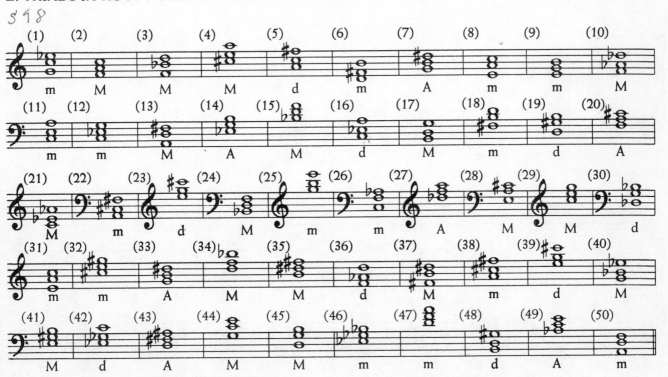

3. FOUR-PART HARMONY IN ROOT POSITION

4. FOUR-PART HARMONY IN ROOT POSITION AND INVERSIONS

5. CHORDS WITH VARYING STRUCTURES AND RANGES

TRIAD-IN-KEY VOCALISES

1. IN MAJOR

Tonic Major 1 3 5 C E G   Dominant Major 5 7 2 G B D

Supertonic minor 2 4 6 d f a   Submediant minor 6 1 3 a c e

Mediant minor 3 5 7 e g b   Leading-Tone diminished 7 2 4 b d f

Subdominant Major 4 6 1 F A C   Tonic Major 1 3 5 3 1

2. IN HARMONIC MINOR

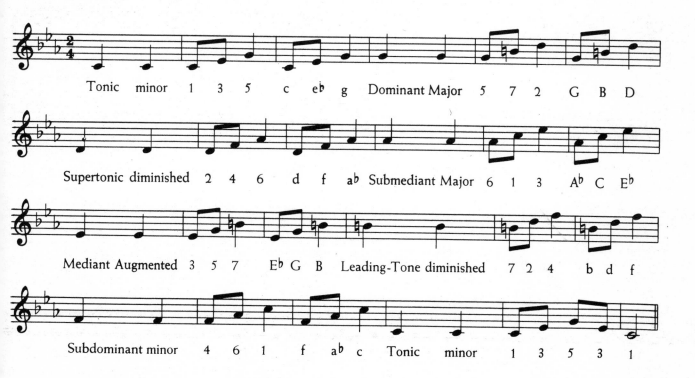

Tonic minor 1 3 5 c eb g   Dominant Major 5 7 2 G B D

Supertonic diminished 2 4 6 d f ab   Submediant Major 6 1 3 Ab C Eb

Mediant Augmented 3 5 7 Eb G B   Leading-Tone diminished 7 2 4 b d f

Subdominant minor 4 6 1 f ab c   Tonic minor 1 3 5 3 1

Selective listening

Two types of *Selective listening* drills are found on the following pages. The TRIAD TYPE IDENTIFICATION drills provide excerpts from music literature to be used for listening selectively for each of the four types of triads. The TRIAD FUNCTION drills consist of prepared progressions intended for introductory drill in listening selectively for triad function.

In the TRIAD TYPE IDENTIFICATION it is important to remember that the objective is to move across the diagram in tempo and place a check mark where the triad type being isolated is heard. The function of the chords in the key is not of significance, and analysis of the chords as tonic, supertonic, or dominant, is not necessary.

As a preparatory drill, review of the appropriate TRIAD VOCALISES (II) is recommended, and, if necessary, preliminary tapping across the diagram in tempo.

A completed TRIAD TYPE IDENTIFICATION drill will appear as shown in the example below. It will be observed that the musical fragment quoted here could be used also for listening selectively for minor triads or for dominant seventh chords. Similarly all of the musical excerpts quoted in this section may be re-used for isolating other chord sonorities. These other chord sonorities are indicated in parentheses above the excerpts for convenience in varied and extensive use of the musical fragments. Multiple diagrams are provided

in the workbook, and more diagrams may be sketched. Additional material for practice in listening for triad types may be found in the SEVENTH CHORD TYPE drills in Chapter 7.

The TRIAD FUNCTION drills are brief, because the technique involved is an integral part of the dictation process and will be practiced whenever harmonic dictation is undertaken. The drill on listening selectively for triad function is included in order to clarify the application of the technique to locating tonic, dominant, subdominant, and other chord functions. As is indicated, each excerpt and its corresponding diagram in the workbook may be used to locate several different chords.

The TRIAD-IN-KEY VOCALISES are valuable in preparation for this drill, but the spelling of each chord in a specific key should be omitted. Singing the vocalise may serve for key establishment, or chords or the scale may be played on the piano; after key establishment the students should be allowed time to review the sound of the chord being sought before the drill begins.

If further introductory drill of this type is needed, material may be taken from the dictation portion of this chapter or from such sources as hymns or patriotic songs. It is necessary to use excerpts which have a simple rhythmic texture and do not modulate.

Performer's copy:

Major triad   Chopin: Nocturne Op. 37, No. 1

Work sheet:

Major triad

TRIAD TYPE IDENTIFICATION

1. MAJOR TRIADS (MINOR TRIADS)

(a) Bach: "Das walt' Gott Vater und Gott Sohn" (adapted)

(b) Bach: "Herzliebster Jesu, was hast du" (adapted)

(c) Dvorak: Symphony No. 5, second movement (adapted)

(d) Brahms: Intermezzo, Op. 118, No. 2 (adapted)

2. MINOR TRIADS (MAJOR AND DIMINISHED TRIADS)

(a) Bach: "Christ, unser Herr, zum Jordan kam" (adapted)

(b) Bach: "Freu' dich sehr, o meine Seele" (adapted)

(c) Christopher Tye: "Come Holy Ghost"

(d) Haydn: String Quartet, Op. 76, No. 4, fourth movement

3. DIMINISHED TRIADS (MAJOR AND MINOR TRIADS)

(a)   Bach: "Vater unser in Himmelreich" (adapted)

(b)   Bach: "Als Jesus Christus in der Nacht" (adapted)

(c)   Brahms: Symphony No. 4 in E minor, fourth movement

(d)   Beethoven: Piano Sonata in Eb major, Op. 7, first movement

4. AUGMENTED TRIADS (MAJOR, MINOR, AND DIMINISHED TRIADS)

(a)   Bach: "Vater unser in Himmelreich" (adapted)

(b)   Bach: "O Ewigkeit, du Donnerwort" (adapted)

(c)   Brahms: Piano Concerto No. 2 in B flat major, Op. 83, fourth movement

Rimsky-Korsakov: *Sadko,* "Song of India"

(d)

TRIAD FUNCTION

1. TONIC, DOMINANT, SUBDOMINANT, SUBMEDIANT, SUPERTONIC

2. TONIC, DOMINANT, SUPERTONIC, LEADING-TONE

3. TONIC, DOMINANT, SUBDOMINANT, SUBMEDIANT, MEDIANT, SUPERTONIC

4. TONIC, DOMINANT, SUBDOMINANT, SUPERTONIC, SUBMEDIANT, LEADING-TONE

Critical listening

The important aspect of ear-training in *Critical listening* is the comparison of what is seen with what is heard. By calling for vocalise formulae in checking work, the instructor may, in effect, hear the student's thought process. If, for example, the student has seen this: and heard this:

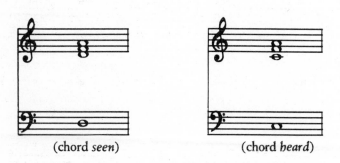

(chord *seen*)   (chord *heard*)

he may make his response by singing the following:*

3 1 5 1 3   5 3 1 3 5
(chord *heard*)   (chord *seen*)

When the *Critical listening* involves a harmonic progression, a preliminary performance of the TRIAD-IN-KEY VOCALISE in the key of the progression will increase efficiency of response by organizing the student's thought on the spelling of chords in that key and preparing his ear for the characteristic sound of those chords.

In most cases the instructor will want to have the student label what he sees before the drill is played. In the case of isolated chords he may simply indicate chord type, or type, soprano position, and inversion. As the chords are played, the student will rewrite and reanalyze any chords that are played differently.

---

*The triad type may be announced by the student in each case, or sung by him on the final tone.

Occasionally the routine may be varied, in the classroom or in a practice session, by making the identification vocally. In this case a student is given the pitch of the chord tone (soprano or bass) which is to remain unchanged. From this tone he vocalises what he sees, then listens to the version which is played, and makes a vocal comparison either to establish that it is the same or to point out the nature of the difference.

In the case of progressions, labelling may consist of Roman numeral analysis only or this may be supplemented by adding chord type and soprano position. As the progressions are played, the student will rewrite and reanalyze any that are played differently. There will be times when the instructor wishes to test the student's ability to discriminate between what is seen and what is heard without any preliminary analysis.

F: I⁶₄   V   I

As was stated in Chapter 5 the exercises appearing now demand some command of the keyboard in order that they may be performed at a reasonable tempo. Although the non-pianist will need to enlist the aid of a pianist for some of his review, it should be observed that the playing of *Critical listening* exercises for review and comparison provides valuable practice in reading at the piano, since complete accuracy is a *sine qua non*.

It will be noted that the early exercises in this section correspond with certain *Basic drills*, whereas the later ones involve harmonic progression and will serve to clarify problems met in the *Dictation* section of this chapter.

Creation of new versions of the later exercises for re-use of the work sheets requires a command of the laws of harmonic progression and voice-leading, and students attempting this should have their versions checked by the instructor before using them in practice sessions.

TRIAD TYPE IDENTIFICATION

1. TRIADS IN ROOT POSITION

(Root unchanged)

(Fifth unchanged)

(Third unchanged)

2. TRIADS IN ROOT POSITION AND INVERSIONS

(Lowest tone unchanged)

(Highest tone unchanged)

3. FOUR-PART HARMONY IN ROOT POSITION
(Bass unchanged)

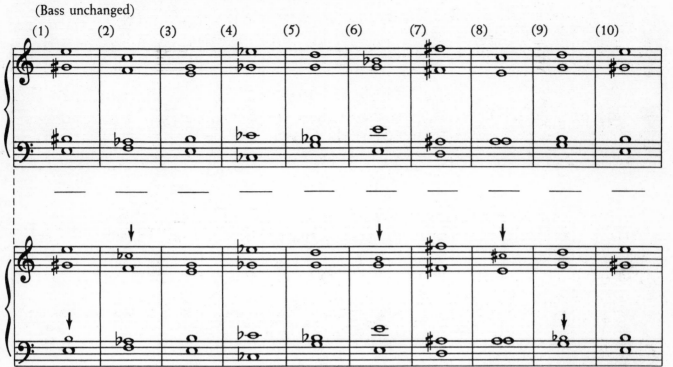

Critical listening

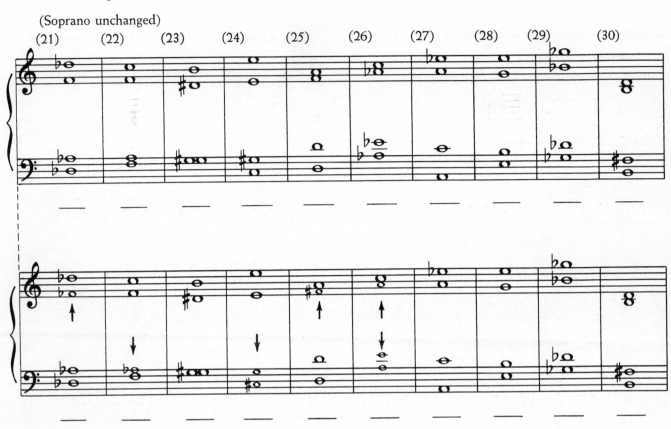

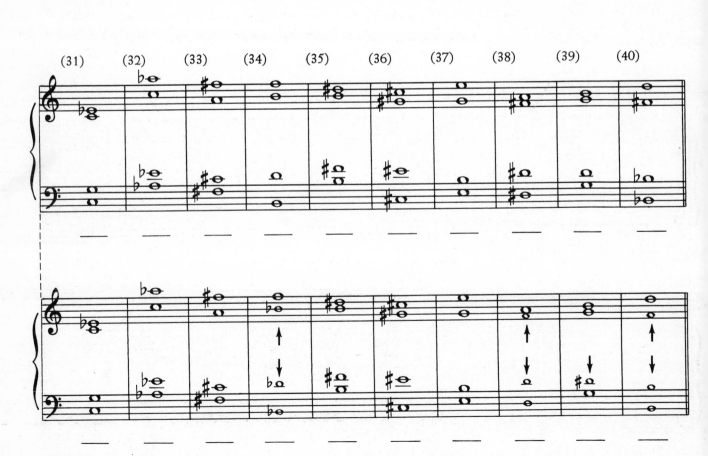

4. FOUR-PART HARMONY IN ROOT POSITION AND INVERSIONS
(Soprano unchanged)

Critical listening

(Bass unchanged)

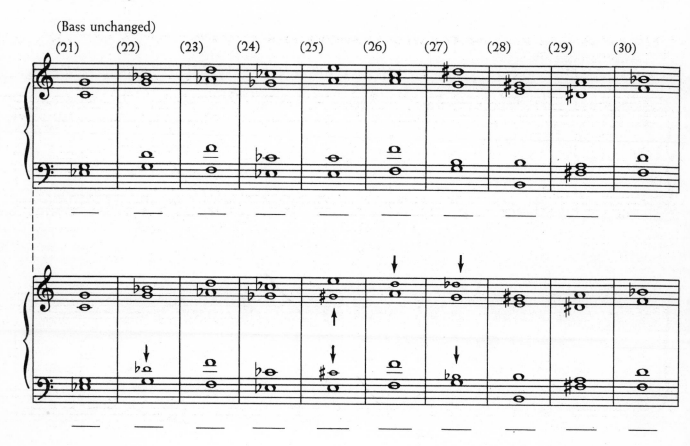

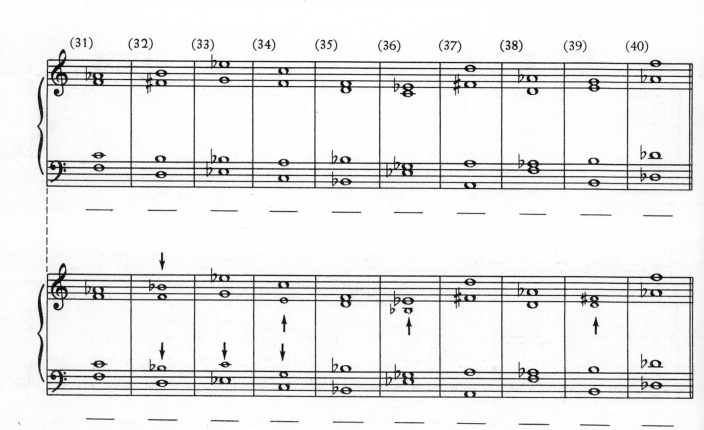

5. CHORDS WITH VARYING STRUCTURES AND RANGES
(Highest tone unchanged)

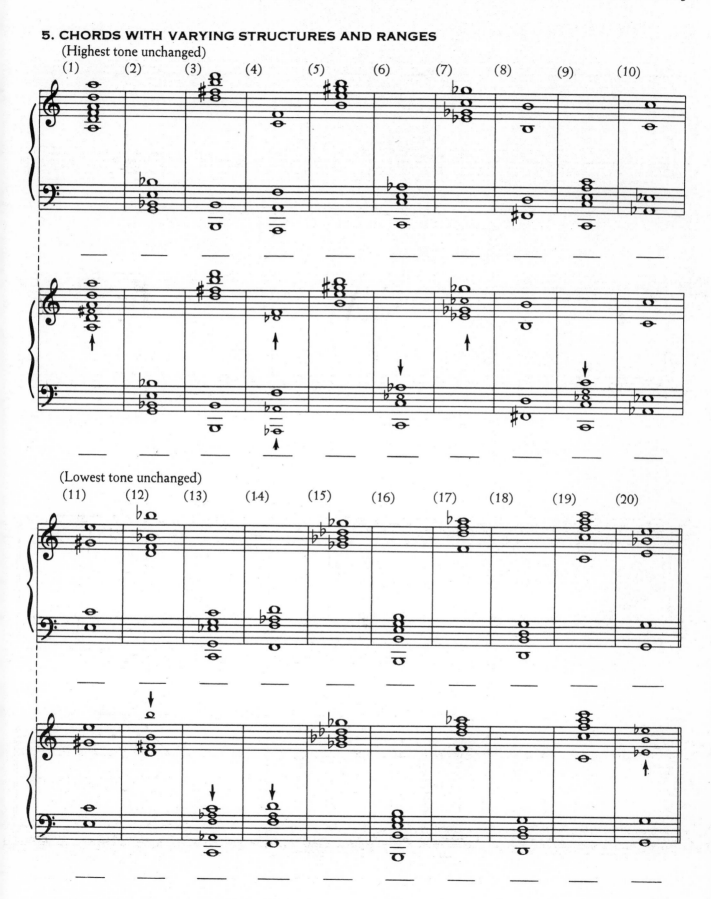

(Lowest tone unchanged)

TWO-CHORD PROGRESSIONS

FOUR-PART HARMONY IN ROOT POSITION

(Soprano unchanged)

HARMONIC PROGRESSIONS

1. FOUR-PART HARMONY IN ROOT POSITION

(Soprano unchanged)

2. FOUR-PART HARMONY IN ROOT POSITION AND INVERSIONS
(Soprano unchanged)

Dictation

Before approaching the taking of dictation of actual music under normal performance conditions, this section provides certain preliminary exercises. The first and most elementary of these is a group of TWO-CHORD PROGRESSIONS involving root position triads only. It is suggested that the necessary key establishment preceding each of these two-chord groups be limited to the playing of the tonic chord or the scale only, since to play a progression would, in some cases, involve the chords in the problem itself.

The next set of preliminary exercises is called CHORD FUNCTION and provides the listener not with the key but with the first chord of the progression, requiring him to have clearly in mind all of the keys to which the given chord belongs diatonically. By proceeding from the given chord to a cadence in each of the keys to which it may belong, the exercises provide an important early insight into the process of modulation by common chord. Because of the limited function of diminished and augmented triads, only major and minor triads are used as the given chords. Usage is limited to that derived from the major and harmonic minor modes. Hence major triads serve as I, IV, and V in major and as V and VI in minor; while minor triads serve as II, III, and VI in major and as I and IV in minor. Root position chords only are used, and it is recommended that all four parts be written out as a means of linking ear-training to basic part-writing technique and demonstrating that success in harmonic dictation may often stem as much from insight into the conventions of harmonic progression and voice-leading as from the ability to make absolute identification of specific pitches. These drills may be transposed to provide practice with many keys.

The HARMONIC PROGRESSIONS are provided to set forth with special clarity certain typical progressions without rhythmic and non-harmonic elements which would obscure them.

Attention is called to the paralleling of *Critical listening* and *Dictation* exercises so that certain problems of recognition and notation may be high-lighted in *Critical listening* before they are approached in *Dictation*.

At the end of this section are several excerpts from literature for dictation which are limited to a triad vocabulary.

LIST OF DICTATION FROM LITERATURE

In the list of dictation material which follows, and in the corresponding lists in Chapters 7 and 8, the nature of cadences and of modulation in each listing will be indicated by the abbreviations given on the next page.

The abbreviation EC, indicating "embellishing chord" will be inserted after certain listings to indicate that they contain, not a clearly defined modulation, but rather a momentary embellishment of one of the chords of the key. Usually the embellishment will be a secondary dominant, but it may embrace a predominant chord as well, or may involve only a chord or chords other than the dominant. The abbreviation EC will indicate any of these possibilities.

In order that these materials may serve the largest number of people effectively, an effort has been made to take a middle-of-the-road position in classifying the musical excerpts in terms of modulation versus embellishment. The author is aware that some users will prefer to analyze without modulation at all in many cases, whereas others will not use the device of embellishing chords. The classification serves merely to provide an index as to the nature of the harmonic material involved, and the actual analysis employed will be that preferred by the individual instructor or school.

Key to Cadence Types

Cad. P. A.	Perfect Authentic (Closed)
Cad. I. A.	Imperfect Authentic (Open)
Cad. H.	Half
Cad. P.	Plagal
Cad. D.	Deceptive

Key to Modulation

Mod. V	Modulation to key of dominant
Mod. IV	Modulation to key of subdominant
Mod. II	Modulation to key of supertonic
Mod. III	Modulation to key of mediant
Mod. VI	Modulation to key of submediant
Mod. VII	Modulation to key of subtonic
Mod. Dist.	Modulation to distantly related key

(Change of mode within same key center is not regarded as modulation)

1. From the 371 Chorales of Bach
   (1) No. 2, mm. 1-4, Cad. P. A., Mod. V
   (2) No. 25, mm. 1-4, Cad. H.
   (3) No. 41, mm. 1-4, Cad. P. A., Mod. VI
   (4) No. 66, mm. 1-4, Cad. P. A., Mod. V
   (5) No. 67, mm. 1-4, Cad. P. A., Mod. V
   (6) No. 102, entire chorale, Cad. P. A., H., Mod. V, II, VI
   (7) No. 143, mm. 1-8, Cad. P., P. A., Mod. V
   (8) No. 167, mm. 1-4, Cad. I. A., P. A.
   (9) No. 177, entire chorale, Cad. P. A., I. A., Mod. IV, VI (EC), V
   (10) No. 209, mm. 1-4, Cad. P. A.
   (11) No. 224, .mm. 1-4, Cad. I. A., P. A., Mod. VI (EC) V

2. Other vocal music
   (1) Purcell: *Dido and Aeneas*, No. 6, "Fear No Danger To Ensue," mm. 1-16 of chorus section, Cad. P. A. (EC)

3. Piano music
   (1) Mussorgsky: *Pictures at an Exhibition*, "The Great Gate of Kiev," mm. 1-8, Cad. H.
   (2) Handel: Suite No. 7, *Sarabande*, mm. 1-8, Cad. H, P. A., Mod. III (EC)
   (3) Mozart: Piano Sonata No. 9 in D major, K. 311, third movement, mm. 1-4, Cad. I. A. (EC)
   (4) Mozart: Piano Sonata No. 17 in D major, K. 576, third movement, mm. 1-4
   (5) D. Scarlatti: Sonata in C, Longo S 2, mm. 1-6, Cad. I. A.
   (6) Bach: French Suite No. 5, Gavotte, mm. 1-4, Cad. I. A.

4. Symphonic music
   (1) Tschaikovsky: *Nutcracker Suite*, March, mm. 1-2
   (2) Beethoven: *Egmont* Overture, mm. 2-5, Cad. P. A.
   (3) Tschaikovsky: "1812" Overture, mm. 1-9, Cad. I. A.
   (4) Brahms: Symphony No. 4, second movement, mm. 5-8 (bi-modal) Cad. P.

5. Musical Excerpts in the *Selective listening* section of this chapter:
   (1) From Triad type identification: 1. (a) and (c); 2. (a) and (c); 3. (a); 4. (c).

TWO-CHORD PROGRESSIONS

FOUR-PART HARMONY IN ROOT POSITION

(Establish key before each progression)

TRIADS · **169**

TRIAD FUNCTION

1. MAJOR TRIADS

(Given: G major triad position of the third, close structure)

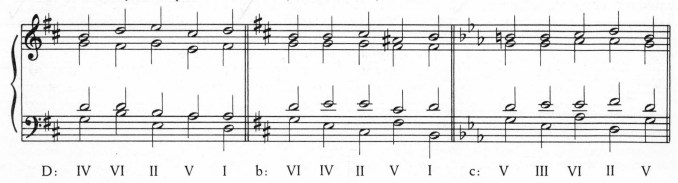

D: IV VI II V I   b: VI IV II V I   c: V III VI II V

G: I VI II V VI   C: V I VI IV I

(Given: A major triad position of the octave, close structure)

A: I VI II V I   E: IV I V VI V   D: V VI II V I

c#: VI IV V I V   d: V I IV V I

2. MINOR TRIADS

(Given: The b minor triad, position of the third, close structure)

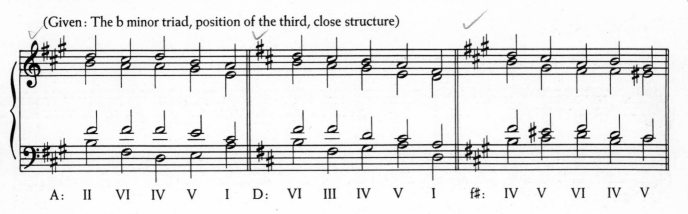

A: II VI IV V I   D: VI III IV V I   f#: IV V VI IV V

b: I IV V V I   G: III IV I V I

(Given: The f minor triad, position of the fifth, open structure)

f: I IV II V VI   Ab: VI IV II V I   Eb: II V VI IV I

Db: III VI II V I   c: IV II V I V

HARMONIC PROGRESSIONS WITH NO MODULATION

1. FOUR-PART HARMONY IN ROOT POSITION

(a)

(b)

(c)

(d)

2. FOUR-PART HARMONY IN ROOT POSITION AND FIRST INVERSION

(a)

3. FOUR-PART HARMONY IN ROOT POSITION, FIRST AND SECOND INVERSION

HARMONIC PROGRESSIONS WITH MODULATION

1. FOUR-PART HARMONY IN ROOT POSITION AND FIRST INVERSION

2. FOUR-PART HARMONY IN ROOT POSITION AND INVERSIONS

(a)

(b)

(c)

(d)

(e)

EXCERPTS FROM LITERATURE

1. SELECTIONS WITH NO MODULATION

Allegro non troppo ma con brio

Brahms: Symphony No. 1 in C minor, fourth movement

Allegro assai

Mozart: Symphony No. 40 in G minor, fourth movement

2. SELECTIONS WITH MODULATION

Moderato

Purcell: *Dido and Aeneas*, "When Monarchs Unite"

Adagio molto semplice e cantabile

Beethoven: Sonata in C minor, Op. 111, second movement

Sight singing

LIST OF SIGHT SINGING FROM LITERATURE

(1) Schubert: *Mass in G*, Kyrie Eleison, mm. 1-28.
(2) Handel: *Messiah*, "Since By Man Came Death," (begin with m. 7).
(3) Handel: *Messiah*, "Worthy Is the Lamb," (begin with m. 7).
(4) Schubert: *Mass in G*, Credo, mm. 1-20.
(5) Mendelssohn: *Elijah*, No. 15, "Cast Thy Burden"
(6) Haydn: *The Creation*, No. 14, "The Heavens Are Telling," (chorus parts)

EXCERPTS FROM LITERATURE

(a)

Lebhaft, doch nicht zu rasch

Brahms: *Deutsche Volkslieder*, No. 18, "der Fiedler"

(b)

Andante moderato

di Lasso: "O Occhi, Manza Mia" from *Libro di Villanelle, Moresche ed Altre Canzoni*

CHAPTER 7

SEVENTH CHORDS

Basic drills

The nomenclature of triads — major, minor, diminished, and augmented — is universal. The same is not true of the nomenclature of seventh chords. Since it is the aim of this book to avoid specialized systems of labelling in order to make the material adaptable for drill accompanying many different teaching programs, the naming of the seventh chord types in the present chapter is an effort to adopt the most widely-used name for each sonority.

The following is a list of the seven diatonic seventh chord types in order of presentation, showing the name used and the construction of the chord in terms of basic triad and size of the interval from root to seventh; also included is a suggested shorthand indication of the types for rapid recording in dictation.

1. Dominant seventh — Major triad, minor seventh — D7
2. Diminished seventh — diminished triad, diminished seventh — d7
3. Half-diminished seventh — diminished triad, minor seventh — ½d7
4. Minor seventh — minor triad, minor seventh — m7
5. Major seventh — Major triad, Major seventh — M7
6. minor-Major seventh — minor triad, Major seventh — mM7
7. Augmented-Major seventh — Augmented triad, Major seventh — AM7

The *Basic drills* consist of SEVENTH CHORD VOCALISES and SEVENTH CHORD TYPE IDENTIFICATION. The SEVENTH CHORD VOCALISES (I) outline the root position chord beginning from each of the four tones of the chord. No verbalization is given with these, but it may be added if desired. The purpose is the same as in the TRIAD VOCALISES, to focus attention on the varying intervallic content of the chords.

The SEVENTH CHORD VOCALISES (II) need little explanation. Here the outlines produce chord degrees in all possible relationships to one another and stress the intervallic relationships existing within the various manifestations of each chord. These outlines will lend themselves especially well to preliminary vocalization and later recognition in the ten-chord groups for *Critical listening* where the unchanged voice may be either soprano or bass. The utmost accuracy in intonation must be stressed.

The SEVENTH CHORD TYPE IDENTIFICATION drills, which progressively add seventh chord types to the basic triad vocabulary may be used as were the TRIAD TYPE IDENTIFICATION drills for type identification only, using the indicated abbreviations, or for identification of type, soprano position and inversion (T, S, B), as described in Chapter 6. As in the case of triads, the recognition process should be made easier by the application of the vocalise patterns to test types and identity of soprano or bass tone. This may be done silently by the student while listening, or vocally as a means of communication of his thinking process when the drill is checked. Here also full notation of the chords may be required, in which case preliminary drill with the corresponding *Critical listening* exercise is recommended.

SEVENTH CHORD VOCALISES I

SEVENTH CHORD VOCALISES II

A. Basic patterns on a single chord.
B. Basic patterns from a single tone.
C. All patterns up from a single tone.
D. All patterns down from a single tone.

1. DOMINANT SEVENTH CHORD

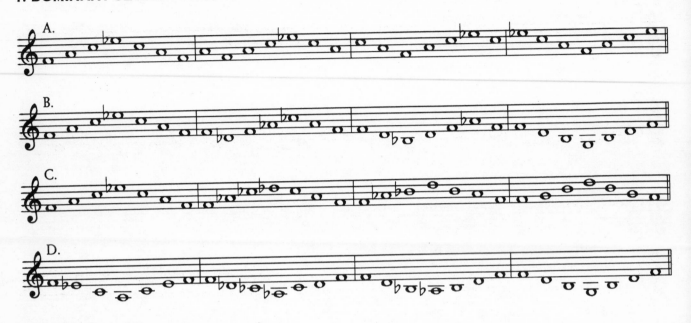

2. DIMINISHED SEVENTH CHORD

3. HALF-DIMINISHED SEVENTH CHORD

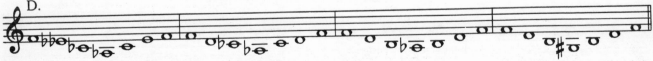

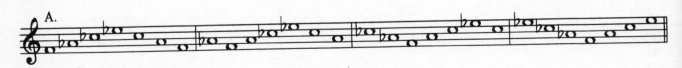

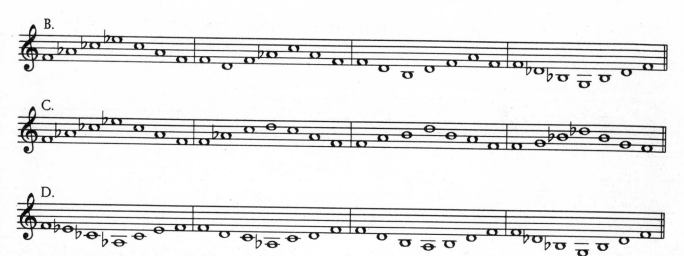

4. MINOR SEVENTH CHORD

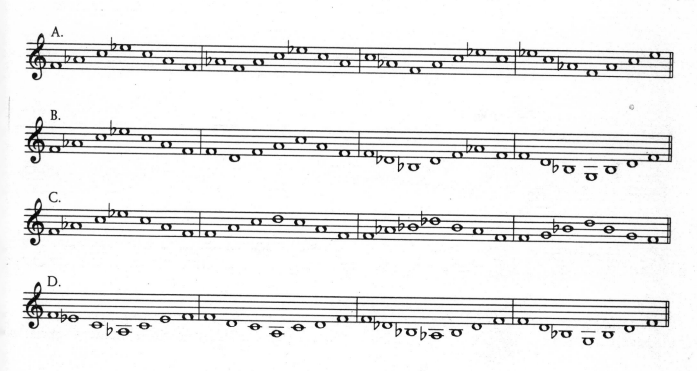

5. MAJOR SEVENTH CHORD

6. MINOR-MAJOR SEVENTH CHORD

7. AUGMENTED-MAJOR SEVENTH CHORD

SEVENTH CHORD TYPE IDENTIFICATION

1. DOMINANT SEVENTH CHORDS AND TRIADS

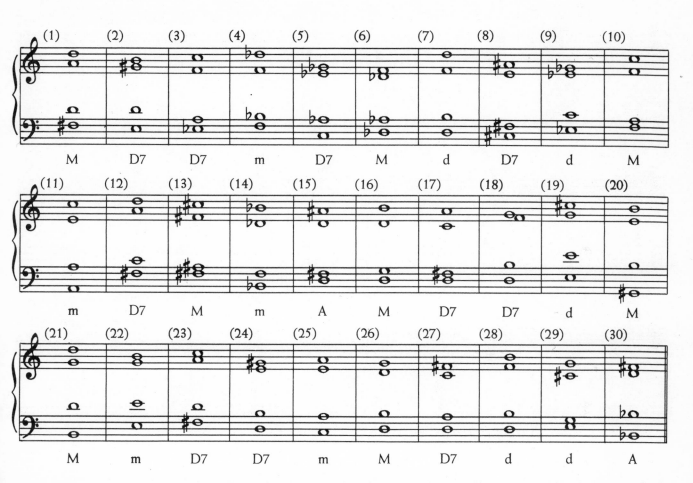

2. DOMINANT AND DIMINISHED SEVENTH CHORDS AND TRIADS

3. DOMINANT, DIMINISHED, AND HALF-DIMINISHED SEVENTH CHORDS AND TRIADS

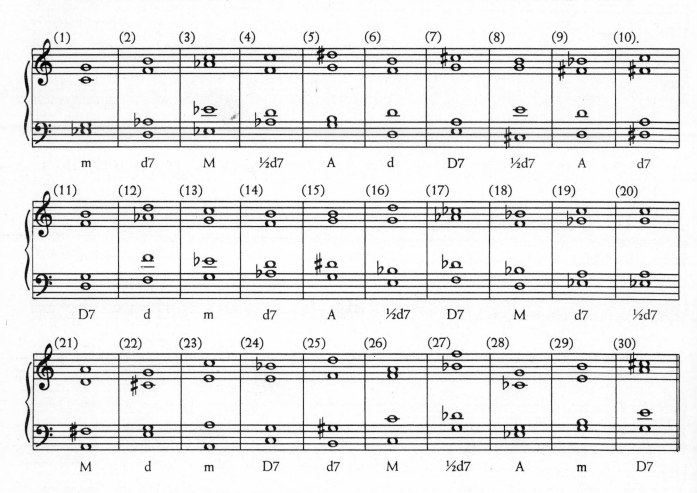

4. DOMINANT, DIMINISHED, HALF-DIMINISHED, AND MINOR SEVENTH CHORDS AND TRIADS

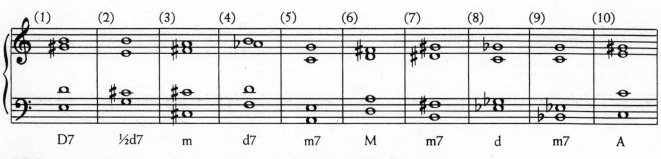

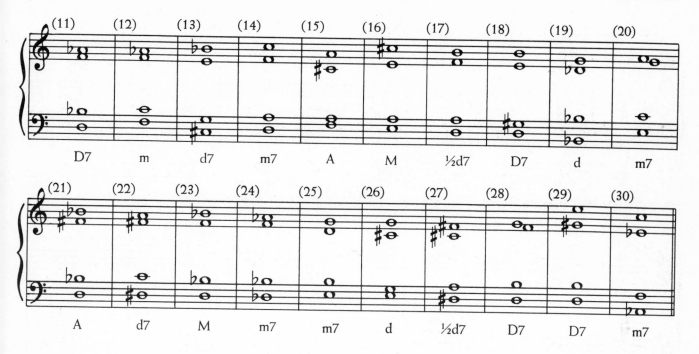

5. DOMINANT, DIMINISHED, HALF-DIMINISHED, MINOR, AND MAJOR SEVENTH CHORDS AND TRIADS

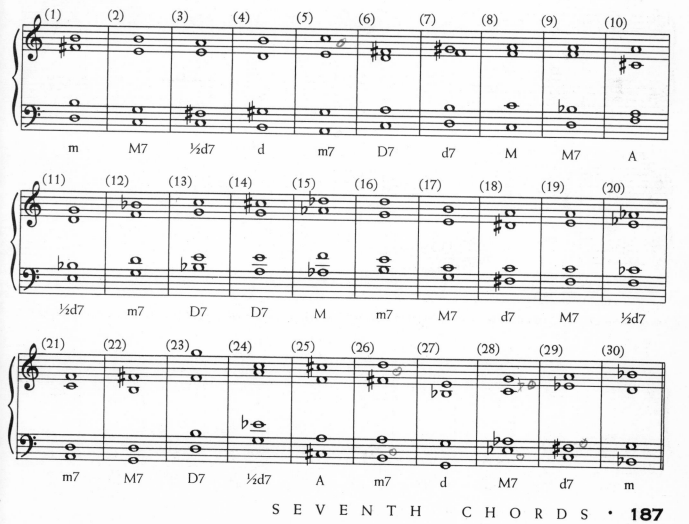

6. ALL SEVENTH CHORDS IN ROOT POSITION

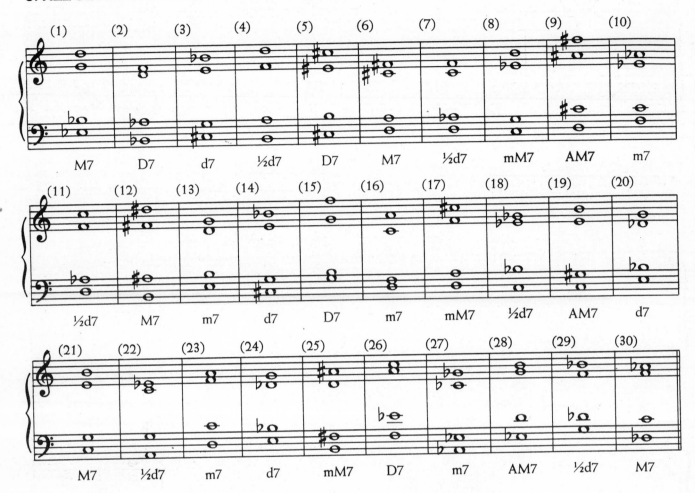

7. ALL SEVENTH CHORDS IN ROOT POSITION AND INVERSIONS

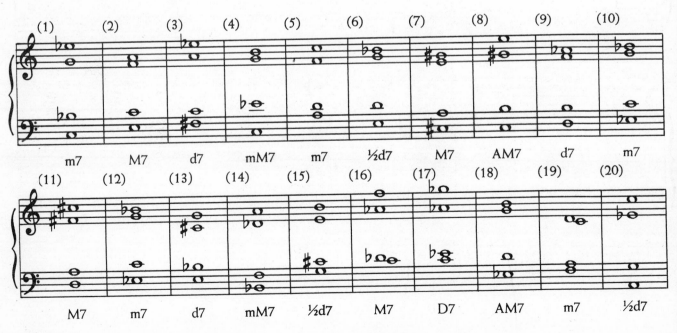

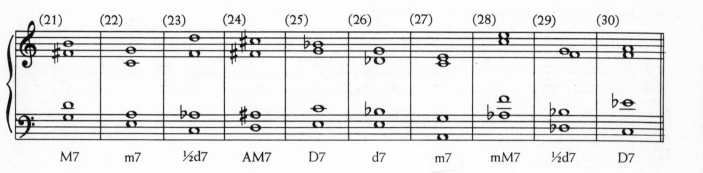

M7   m7   ½d7   AM7   D7   d7   m7   mM7   ½d7   D7

8. ALL SEVENTH CHORDS WITH VARYING STRUCTURES AND RANGES

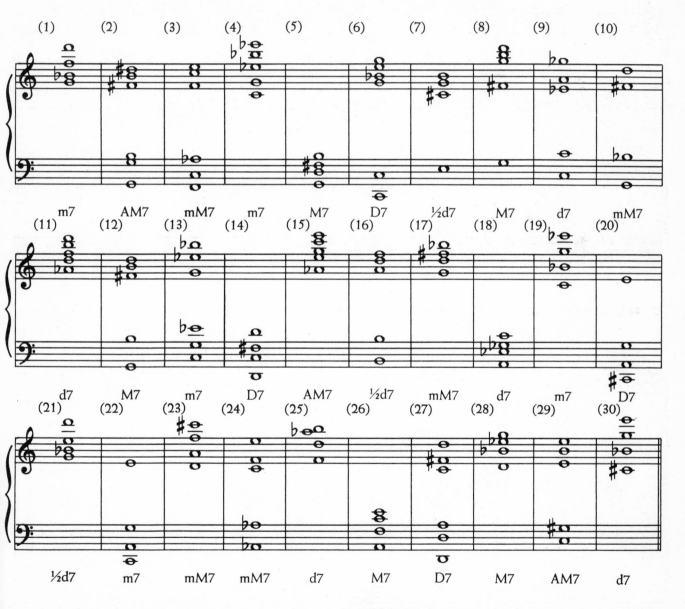

Selective listening

As in previous *Selective listening* exercises, the objective here is to move across the diagram in tempo and place a check mark where the seventh chord type being isolated is heard. Three exercises are given for each of the main types of seventh chords. It will be readily apparent that these musical fragments may be used to isolate various triad and seventh chord sounds in addition to the chord under which they are listed. Other prevalent or strategically located triads and seventh chords included in the excerpts are indicated in parenthesis above the excerpt. It is hoped that by this time the instructor and students are creating impromptu *Selective listening* drills in connection with numerous problems in dictation and aural analysis.

Review of the appropriate SEVENTH CHORD VOCALISES is recommended in order to prepare for recognition of each seventh chord sonority in any soprano position and inversion.

SEVENTH CHORD TYPE IDENTIFICATION
(DERIVED FROM THE CHORALES OF J. S. BACH)

1. DOMINANT SEVENTH CHORD

(a) (MAJOR TRIADS IN FIRST INVERSION, MINOR SEVENTH CHORD)

"Du Friedensfurst"

(b) (MINOR TRIADS IN ROOT POSITION AND FIRST INVERSION)

"Kommt her zu mir"

(c) (DIMINISHED SEVENTH CHORD)

"Herzliebster Jesu, was hast du verbrochen"

2. DIMINISHED SEVENTH CHORD

(a) (DOMINANT SEVENTH CHORD, MINOR TRIADS)

"Herzlich tut mich verlangen"

(b) **(MAJOR AND MINOR TRIADS IN ROOT POSITION AND FIRST INVERSION)**

"O Traurigkeit"

(c) **(MINOR TRIADS)**

"Warum betrubst du dich"

3. HALF-DIMINISHED SEVENTH CHORD

(a) **(MAJOR TRIADS)**

"Das Neugeborne Kindelein"

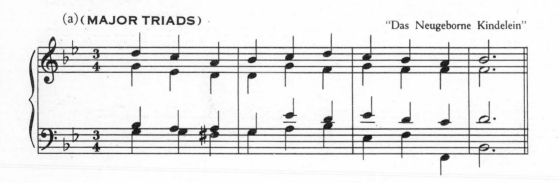

(b) **(DOMINANT SEVENTH CHORD)**

"Vom Himmel Hoch"

(c) (MAJOR AND MINOR TRIADS)

"Erbarm' dich mein"

4. MINOR SEVENTH CHORD

(a) (DOMINANT SEVENTH CHORD)

"Wenn mein Stundlein vorhanden ist"

(b) (TRIADS IN FIRST INVERSION)

"Werde munter, mein Gemute"

(c) (MAJOR AND MINOR TRIADS)

"Valet will ich dir geben"

5. MAJOR SEVENTH CHORD

(a) (DIMINISHED SEVENTH CHORD)

"Jesus Christus, unser Heiland"

(b) (DOMINANT SEVENTH CHORD, DIMINISHED SEVENTH CHORD)

"Vater unser im Himmelreich"

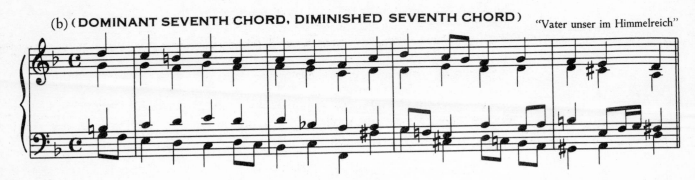

(c) (MINOR SEVENTH CHORD, MAJOR TRIADS)

"In allen meinen Taten"

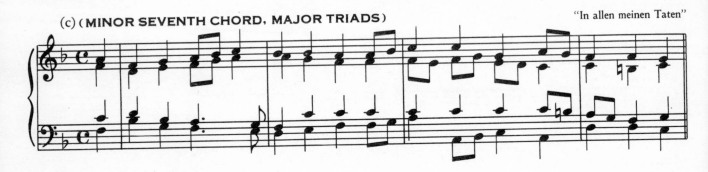

Critical listening

The early drills in this section parallel the SEVENTH CHORD TYPE IDENTIFICATION drills in the *Basic drills* section and may be used effectively in conjunction with them, while the later drills, involving harmonic progression, will serve as preparation for *Dictation*.

Observations made in the *Critical listening* section of Chapter 6 concerning use of vocalises, labelling of chords, and reviewing of completed exercises apply equally here and should be reread at this time. The abbreviations for the seventh chord types given at the beginning of the present chapter may be used in labelling.

Varying of errors in re-use of the later exercises and work sheets demands considerable skill in part-writing, and students should make sure of the correctness of their chord choice and voice-leading before using new versions in practice sessions.

SEVENTH CHORD TYPE IDENTIFICATION

1. DOMINANT SEVENTH CHORDS AND TRIADS

(Soprano unchanged)

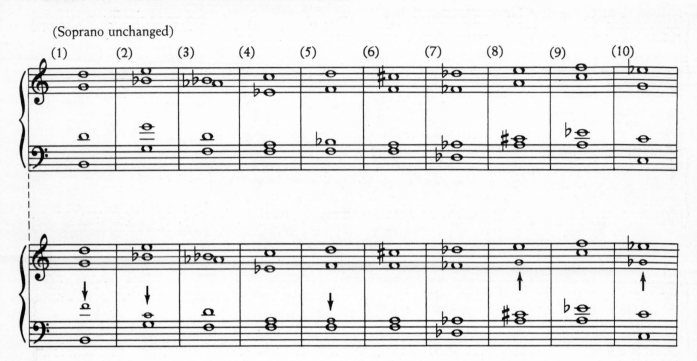

(Bass unchanged)

2. DOMINANT AND DIMINISHED SEVENTH CHORDS AND TRIADS
(Soprano unchanged)

(Bass unchanged)

3. DOMINANT, DIMINISHED, AND HALF-DIMINISHED SEVENTH CHORDS AND TRIADS
(Soprano unchanged)

4. DOMINANT, DIMINISHED, HALF-DIMINISHED, AND MINOR SEVENTH CHORDS AND TRIADS

5. DOMINANT, DIMINISHED, HALF-DIMINISHED, MINOR, AND MAJOR SEVENTH CHORDS AND TRIADS

(Soprano unchanged)

(Bass unchanged)

6. ALL SEVENTH CHORDS AND TRIADS

(Soprano unchanged)

(Bass unchanged)

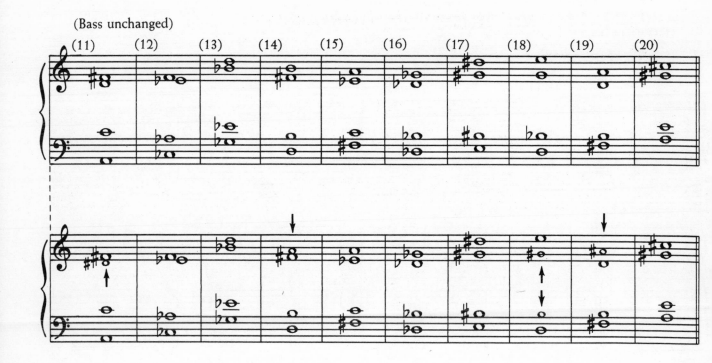

HARMONIC PROGRESSIONS

1. DOMINANT SEVENTH CHORDS AND TRIADS

(Soprano unchanged)

2. DIATONIC AND SECONDARY DOMINANT SEVENTH CHORDS AND TRIADS

(Soprano unchanged)

3. DOMINANT AND DIMINISHED SEVENTH CHORDS AND TRIADS

(Soprano unchanged)

4. DOMINANT, DIMINISHED, AND HALF-DIMINISHED SEVENTH CHORDS AND TRIADS

(Soprano unchanged)

5. DOMINANT, DIMINISHED, HALF-DIMINISHED, AND MINOR SEVENTH CHORDS AND TRIADS

(Soprano unchanged)

6. DOMINANT, DIMINISHED, HALF-DIMINISHED, MINOR AND MAJOR SEVENTH CHORDS AND TRIADS

(Soprano unchanged)

7. ALL SEVENTH CHORDS AND TRIADS

(Soprano unchanged)

Dictation

The device of CHORD FUNCTION drills, first encountered in Chapter 6, reappears here applied to those seventh chord types capable of a variety of diatonic functions.

Because it is assumed that the student who is equipped with a harmonic vocabulary as rich as that involved in this chapter is able to deal with some degree of rhythmic complexity and use of non-harmonicism, no further contrived exercises are provided, and instructor and student will draw dictation material from the quoted excerpts and lists provided and from sources of their own choosing. Discovering pertinent material is an important part of the learning process.

LIST OF DICTATION FROM LITERATURE

(See page 168 for list of abbreviations used)

1. Dominant seventh chord
   A. From the 371 Chorales of Bach:
      (1) No. 32, mm. 1-4, Cad. P., P. A.
      (2) No. 85, mm. 1-4, Cad. H (on IV), P. A. (EC)
      (3) No. 103, entire chorale, Cad. I. A., H., P. A., Mod. II (EC)
      (4) No. 107, mm. 1-7, Cad. P., H (on III), P. A. (EC)
      (5) No. 360, mm. 1-2, Cad. D., P. A.
   B. Other vocal music:
      (1) Verdi: *Requiem*, Offertorio, "Hostias," mm. 120-129 (or 139) Cad. I. A., P. A.
      (2) Haydn: *The Creation*, No. 2, "In the Beginning" (chorus part), Cad. I. A., P. A., Mod. VI
      (3) Haydn: *The Creation*, No. 3, second section of chorus, "A New Created World," Cad. P. A. (EC)
   C. Piano music:
      (1) Beethoven: Piano Sonata No. 7 in D major, Op. 10, No. 3, third movement, mm. 1-16, Cad. H, P. A., Mod. II
      (2) Beethoven: Piano Sonata No. 3 in C major, Op. 2, No. 3, second movement, mm. 1-4, Cad. H
      (3) Schubert: Impromptu, Op. 142, No. 2, mm. 1-16, Cad. I. A., P. A. (EC)
      (4) Schubert: Sonata in A major, Op. posth., first movement, mm. 55-64, Cad. H. Mod. Dist.
   D. Chamber music:
      (1) Beethoven: String Quartet in A major, Op. 18, No. 5, third movement, mm. 1-16, Cad. H., P. A. (EC)
      (2) Mozart: String Quartet, K. 421, second movement, mm. 1-8, Cad. I. A., P. A., Mod. V
   E. Symphonic music:
      (1) Beethoven: Symphony No. 6 in F major, first movement, mm. 1-16, Cad. H.
   F. From *Selective listening*:
      (1) Chapter 6, TRIAD TYPE IDENTIFICATION, 1. (b) and 2. (b)
      (2) Chapter 7, SEVENTH CHORD TYPE IDENTIFICATION, 1. (b)

2. Diminished seventh chord
   A. From the 371 Chorales of Bach:
      (1) No. 24, mm. 1-4, Cad. P., P. A. (EC)
      (2) No. 321, entire chorale, Cad. D., P. A., H., I. A., Mod. VII (EC)
      (3) No. 340, mm. 1-4, Cad. I. A., P. A., Mod. III, V (EC)
   B. Piano music:
      (1) Beethoven: Piano Sonata No. 10 in G major, Op. 14, No. 2, second movement, mm. 1-16, Cad. H., I. A., P. A., Mod. V (IV) (EC)
      (2) Mozart: Piano Sonata No. 17 in D major, K. 576, second movement, mm. 1-16, Cad. H., P. A. (EC) (record analysis only)
      (3) Beethoven: Piano Sonata No. 8 in C minor, Op. 13, first movement, mm. 1-3
      (4) Beethoven: Piano Sonata No. 7 in D major, Op. 10, No. 3, second movement, mm. 1-9, Cad. I. A., P. A., Mod. IV (EC)
   C. Chamber music:
      (1) Beethoven: String Quartet, Op. 59, No. 2, second movement, mm. 1-8, Cad. H., P. A. (EC)
   D. Symphonic music:
      (1) Brahms: *Academic Festival Overture*, mm. 1-7, Cad. P. A., Mod. V.
      (2) Tschaikovsky: Symphony No. 5 in E minor, fourth movement, mm. 1-10, Cad. H. (EC)
   E. From *Selective listening*:
      (1) Chapter 6, TRIAD TYPE IDENTIFICATION, 4. (b)
      (2) Chapter 7, SEVENTH CHORD TYPE IDENTIFICATION, 1. (c); 2. (a), (b), and (c); 5. (a) and (b)

3. Half-diminished seventh chord
   A. From the 371 Chorales of Bach:
      (1) No. 58, mm. 1-4, Cad. P., I. A., Mod. III (EC)
      (2) No. 166, mm. 1-6, Cad. I. A., H., P. A. (EC)
      (3) No. 338, mm. 1-4, Cad. H., P. A. (EC)
   B. Piano music:
      (1) Schubert: Piano Sonata in E♭ major, Op. 122, second movement, mm. 1-8, Cad. H., P. A., Mod. III (EC)
      (2) Bach: English Suite No. 6, Sarabande, mm. 1-8, Cad. H. (EC)
   C. Chamber music:
      (1) Haydn: String Quartet, Op. 64, No. 5, second movement, mm. 1-8, Cad. I. A., H. (EC)
   D. Symphonic music:
      (1) Brahms: Symphony No. 3 in F major, second movement, mm. 1-6, Cad. I. A. (EC)
      (2) Tschaikovsky: Symphony No. 4 in F minor, second movement, mm. 1-9, Cad. H.
      (3) Tschaikovsky: Symphony No. 5 in E minor, first movement, mm. 1-10, Cad. H. (EC)
   E. From *Selective listening*:
      (1) Chapter 6, TRIAD TYPE IDENTIFICATION, 3. (b); 4. (b)
      (2) Chapter 7, SEVENTH CHORD TYPE IDENTIFICATION, 3. (a)

4. Minor seventh chord
   A. From the 371 Chorales of Bach:
      (1) No. 62, mm. 1-4, Cad. H., P. A., Mod. III
      (2) No. 101, mm. 1-4, Cad. D., P. A., Mod. VI
      (3) No. 106, entire chorale, Cad. H., P. A., I. A., Mod. VI, V (EC)
      (4) No. 108, entire chorale, Cad. I. A., P. A., H. (on VI), Mod. VI, V (EC)
   B. Piano music:
      (1) Beethoven: Piano Sonata No. 18 in E♭ major, Op. 31, No. 3, first
          movement, mm. 1-8, Cad. P. A. (EC)
      (2) Beethoven: Piano Sonata No. 14 in C♯ minor, Op. 27, No. 2, second
          movement, mm. 1-8, Cad. P. A. (EC)
      (3) Schubert: Impromptu, Op. 90, No. 1, mm. 6-9, Cad. P. A.
   C. Chamber music:
      (1) Haydn: String Quartet, Op. 20, No. 4, second movement, mm. 1-8,
          Cad. P. A., Mod. III
      (2) Haydn: String Quartet, Op. 20, No. 5, third movement, mm. 1-8, Cad.
          I. A., P. A. (EC)
   D. Symphonic music:
      (1) Beethoven: Symphony No. 9 in D minor, third movement, mm. 3-19,
          Cad. H., I. A., P. A. (EC)
   E. From *Selective listening*:
      (1) Chapter 6, Triad type identification, 3. (b)
      (2) Chapter 7, Seventh chord type identification, 1. (a), 4. (b) and (c)

5. Major seventh chord
   A. From the 371 Chorales of Bach:
      (1) No. 17, entire chorale, Cad. P. A., I. A., Mod. IV, V, VII, III (EC)
      (2) No. 346, mm. 1-6, Cad. H., I. A., P. A., Mod. III
      (3) No. 359, entire chorale, Cad. P. A., I. A., H., Mod. VI, II (EC)
   B. Other vocal music:
      (1) Handel: *Messiah*, "Worthy Is the Lamb," mm. 1-7 (voice parts),
          Cad. H., Mod. VI
   C. Piano music:
      (1) Bach: Well-tempered Clavier, Book I, Prelude in C major (record
          bass line and analysis, using entire prelude or mm. 1-11), Cad. I. A.,
          H., Mod. V (EC)
   D. Symphonic music:
      (1) Bizet: *L'Arlesienne, Suite* No. 1, "Minuetto," mm. 1-9, Cad. I. A.
   E. From *Selective listening*:
      (1) Chapter 6, Triad type identification, 4. (a)
      (2) Chapter 7, Seventh chord type identification, 5. (a), (b), and (c)

6. Minor-major seventh chord
   A. Piano music:
      (1) Bach: Well-tempered Clavier, Book I, Prelude in C♯ minor, mm. 1-8,
          Cad. H., I. A.
   B. Symphonic music:
      (1) Tschaikovsky: Symphony No. 4 in F minor, second movement, mm.
          10-21, Cad. H., P. A.

7. Augmented-major seventh chord
   A. From the 371 Chorales of Bach:
      (1) No. 15, entire chorale, Cad. P. A., I. A., D., Mod. V, III (EC)
      (2) No. 71, entire chorale, Cad. H., P., P. A., D., Mod. III, VII, IV (EC)
      (3) No. 338, entire chorale, Cad. H., P. A., Mod. VI (EC)
   B. Other vocal music:
      (1) Schumann: "Ich Grolle Nicht," Op. 48, No. 7, mm. 1-12, Cad. I. A. (EC)
   C. Piano music:
      (1) Chopin: Mazurka, Op. 68, No. 2, mm. 17-24, Cad. I. A., P. A., Mod. VI
   D. Chamber music:
      (1) Beethoven: String Quartet, Op. 18, No. 1, second movement, mm. 1-9, Cad. H. (EC)

SEVENTH CHORD FUNCTION

1. HALF-DIMINISHED SEVENTH CHORD

(The A half-diminished 7th chord, root position)

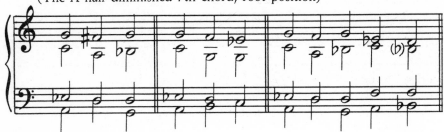

(The C# half-diminished 7th chord, first inversion)

(The G half-diminished 7th chord, second inversion)

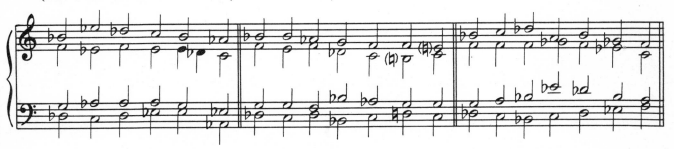

2. MINOR SEVENTH CHORD

(The C minor seventh chord, root position)

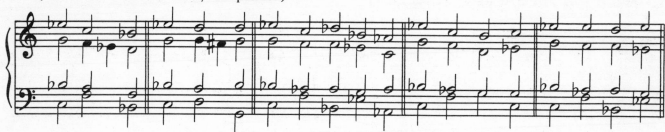

(The F♯ minor seventh chord, first inversion)

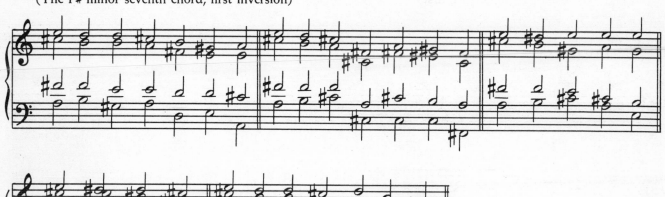

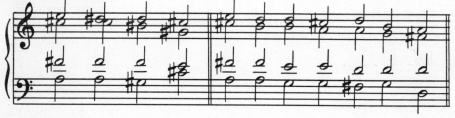

(The D minor seventh chord, third inversion)

3. MAJOR SEVENTH CHORD

(The G major seventh chord, root position)

(The E flat major seventh chord, first inversion)

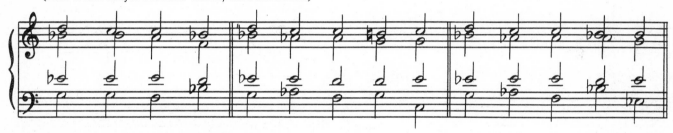

(The A major seventh chord, second inversion)

EXCERPTS FROM LITERATURE

1. DOMINANT SEVENTH CHORD

Tschaikovsky: *Album for the Young*, Op. 39, "Morning Prayer"

Lento

Beethoven: Symphony No. 1 in C major, first movement

Adagio molto

2. DIMINISHED SEVENTH CHORD

Mozart: *Requiem*, "Domine Jesu"

Andante

Andante cantabile

Beethoven: String Quartet in A major, Op. 18, No. 5, third movement

3. HALF-DIMINISHED SEVENTH CHORD

Allegretto

Schubert: Sonata in A major, Op. posth., fourth movement

Moderato

Mozart: String Quartet in B flat major, K. 458, second movement

4. MINOR SEVENTH CHORD

Allegro maestoso, ma moderato

Mendelssohn: *Elijah*, "Be Not Afraid"

Allegro molto moderato

Schubert: Impromptu, Op. 90, No. 1

5. MAJOR SEVENTH CHORD

Handel: *Messiah*, "Surely He Hath Borne Our Griefs"

Bach: Fantasie in A minor

6. MINOR-MAJOR SEVENTH CHORD

Tschaikovsky: Symphony No. 5 in E minor, first movement

7. AUGMENTED-MAJOR SEVENTH CHORD

Larghetto con gran espressione

Bach: *Magnificat,* "Et Misericordia"

Sight singing

LIST OF SIGHT SINGING FROM LITERATURE

(1) Mozart: *Requiem Mass*, "Agnus Dei"
(2) Mozart: *Ave Verum Corpus*, K. 618
(3) Mendelssohn: *Elijah*, No. 24, "Woe To Him"

EXCERPTS FROM LITERATURE

Allegro risoluto

Verdi: *Requiem*, "Libera Me."

Grave

Mendelssohn: *Elijah*, "Yet Doth the Lord See It Not"

CHAPTER 8

Altered Chords

No specific *Basic drills* are provided for altered chords. The altered chord vocabulary drilled in this chapter includes only one chord, the augmented six-four-three or French sixth, which has a sound unique from the chord types in the diatonic vocabulary. The other chords included and their equivalent sonorities are:

Augmented sixth chord (Italian sixth) — Dominant seventh (omitted fifth)

Augmented six-five chord (German sixth) — Dominant seventh (complete)

Doubly augmented fourth chord — Dominant seventh (complete)[1]

Neapolitan sixth chord — Major triad

These chords may be distinguished from their diatonic counterparts aurally by their resolution and, in the case of the augmented sixth chords, visually by their spelling. Practice in these techniques is provided by *Selective listening* and *Critical listening*.

The chromatically altered chords produced by bi-modal or secondary dominant effects have been included in music lists of earlier chapters because of the essentially diatonic function they maintain. Further chromaticism beyond these chords and the chords of the present chapter tends to be apprehended more in terms of its linear tendencies than of the effect of the vertical sonority; for this reason we proceed no further in drilling specific altered chords.

---

[1] This chord is an enharmonically re-spelled German sixth chord wherein the raised second scale degree is substituted for the minor third degree in order to resolve correctly to the major third degree in the major tonic six-four chord. Many authors do not list this chord since composers such as Beethoven, Mozart and Schubert did not alter the conventional German sixth spelling in order to avoid the uncharacteristic chromatic movement. It is included here for two reasons: some widely-used harmony texts do include it in the altered chord roster; and the problem of listening for the tell-tale resolution to major tonic six-four in order to choose between the two spellings helps to form the habit of intense focusing of attention which is being sought throughout this course of study.

Selective listening

As the harmonic vocabulary grows richer, the *Selective listening* process grows easier, and the student will find that the tension-producing chromaticism of the group of chords under study makes them stand out vividly from diatonic chords surrounding them. For this reason only a brief *Selective listening* drill is provided with the present chapter; however, the process of listening selectively should be habitual by this stage, and the student should react in this way to any excerpt containing one of these chromatic structures.

ALTERED CHORD TYPE IDENTIFICATION

1. NEAPOLITAN SIXTH CHORD

Mendelssohn: *Variations sérieuses* in D minor, No. 16

2. ITALIAN SIXTH CHORD

Beethoven: Piano Sonata No. 3 in C major, Op. 2, No. 3, first movement

3. GERMAN SIXTH CHORD

Sibelius: *Finlandia*

4. FRENCH SIXTH CHORD

Beethoven: Piano Sonata No. 4 in E♭ major, Op. 7, second movement

Critical listening

It was observed earlier that with one exception the vocabulary introduced in the present chapter is identical in sound with structures previously studied; therefore, groups of isolated chords for type identification are not a practical method of drill and did not appear as *Basic drills*.

On the other hand, groups of isolated chords for critical listening make an especially useful type of drill, since they foster the association of the familiar dominant seventh sonority with the exceptional notation of the augmented sixth chord types having that sound. In these exercises, the student should first analyze the given chords, then, as they are played, rewrite and reanalyze any chords that are played differently. These chords should be used and re-used with new variants until the sound of these new structures is firmly linked with their written appearance. A similar procedure is recommended for the harmonic progressions with altered chords which follow. A review of the discussion at the beginning of the *Critical listening* section of Chapter 6 is suggested at this time.

ALTERED CHORD TYPE IDENTIFICATION

(Soprano unchanged)

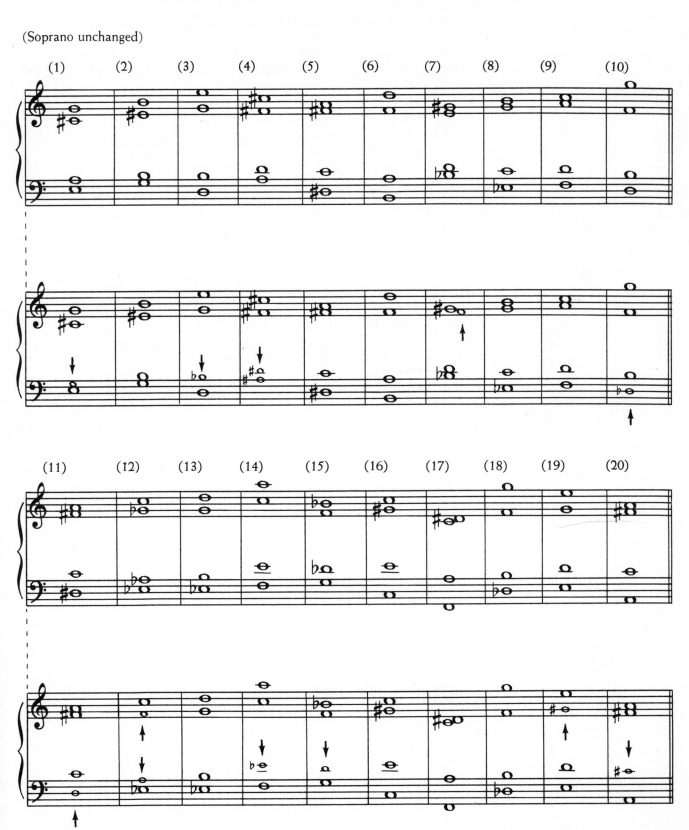

(Bass unchanged)

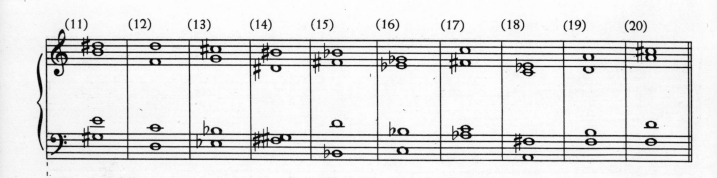

HARMONIC PROGRESSIONS

(Soprano unchanged)

Dictation

The ALTERED CHORD FUNCTION drills which open this dictation section differ from their counterparts in Chapters 6 and 7 in that they proceed, not from a given first chord, but from only the outside voices of the first chord. These outside voices are to be filled in with either a true dominant seventh chord, with one of the three augmented sixth chords which sound like the dominant seventh, or with the unique-sounding French sixth chord.

After the class or practice group has been given the two tones (with the alternative spellings of the upper tone as minor seventh or augmented sixth), time should be allowed for determining the keys which will be involved and the spellings of the five possible chords. Here, as in previous CHORD FUNCTION drills, writing all four parts at dictation is recommended in order to link the listening process with the foreknowledge of normal and predictable voice leading.

The ALTERED CHORD FUNCTION drills may be transposed and assembled in new combinations, and new progressions may be modeled on these so as to provide as much additional practice or testing material as is needed.

The quoted and listed dictation material from actual literature is classified according to altered chord content. The excerpts are from standard literature, as was explained in the Introduction, but with the richness of the vocabulary now involved it is assumed more than ever that students and instructors will seek new material, drawn whenever possible from music being studied in other courses, in order that the ear-training phase may be closely related to the total learning process in the music curriculum. Creativity may be stimulated by requiring the students to compose phrases and period forms to be dictated to the class.

LIST OF DICTATION FROM LITERATURE

1. The Neapolitan sixth chord
   A. From the 371 Chorales of Bach:
      (1) No. 262, mm. 1-4, Cad. H., P. A., (EC)
   B. Other vocal music:
      (1) Schubert: *Mass in G*, Kyrie Eleison, mm. 16-28 (voice parts) Cad. H., I. A., P. A., Mod. IV, II
      (2) Schubert: "Die Krähe," mm. 1-5, Cad. P. A. (EC)
      (3) Bach: *St. Matthew Passion*, No. 40, "He Holds His Peace," Cad. P. A., Mod. IV, V
   C. Piano music:
      (1) Mussorgsky: *Pictures at an Exhibition*, "Bydlo," mm. 1-10, Cad P.
      (2) Chopin: Mazurka, Op. 7, No. 2, mm. 1-16, Cad. I. A., P. A., D., Mod. V (EC)
      (3) Beethoven: Piano Sonata No. 14 in C♯ minor, Op. 27, No. 2, first movement, mm. 43-51, Cad. P. A., Mod. III
      (4) Bach: French Suite No. 1, Sarabande, mm. 1-8, Cad. H (EC)
      (5) Chopin: Waltz, Op. 34, No. 2, mm. 69-76, Cad. D., H
   D. Concerto:
      (1) Mozart: Piano Concerto No. 23 in A major, K. 488, second movement, mm. 1-12, Cad. H., P. A.

2. The Italian sixth chord
   A. From the 371 Chorales of Bach:
      (1) No. 19, mm. 1-4, Cad. H., P. A. (EC)
      (2) No. 216, entire chorale, Cad. H., I. A., P. A., Mod. III, V, VI (EC)

B. Piano music:
    (1) Tschaikovsky: *Album for the Young*, Op. 39, "Mazurka," mm. 1-16, Cad. H., Mod. III
    (2) Beethoven: Piano Sonata No. 21 in C major, Op. 53, second movement introduction, mm. 1-9, Cad. H., P. A. (EC)
    (3) Beethoven: Piano Sonata No. 26 in E♭ major, Op. 81a, first movement, mm. 1-4, Cad. H (EC)
    (4) Beethoven: Piano Sonata No. 24 in F♯ major, Op. 78, second movement, mm. 1-12, Cad. H., I. A., Mod. IV (EC)

C. Chamber music:
    (1) Haydn: String quartet, Op. 17, No. 1, third movement, mm. 1-10, Cad. H., P. A. (also involves Neapolitan sixth and transient effect of German sixth)

D. Symphonic music:
    (1) Beethoven: Symphony No. 5, first movement, mm. 6-21, Cad. H
    (2) Beethoven: *Prometheus* Overture, mm. 1-4, Cad. H. (EC)

3. The German sixth chord
  A. From the 371 Chorales of Bach:
    No. 340, entire chorale, Cad. I. A., P. A., H., Mod. III, V (EC)
  B. Piano music:
    (1) Tschaikovsky: *Album for the Young*, Op. 39, "A Winter Morning," mm. 1-16, Cad. H., I. A., Mod. VI (involves Italian sixth also)
    (2) Beethoven: Piano Sonata No. 30 in E major, Op. 109, third movement, mm. 1-16, Cad. H., P. A., Mod. III
    (3) Beethoven: Piano Sonata No. 23 in F minor, Op. 57, second movement, mm. 1-8, Cad. I. A., P. A.
    (4) Schubert: Sonata in C minor, Op. posth., first movement, mm. 1-8, Cad. H (EC)
    (5) Beethoven: Thirty-two Variations, C minor, theme, Cad. P. A. (EC)
  C. Chamber music:
    (1) Haydn: String quartet, Op. 74, No. 2, second movement, mm. 1-8, Cad. H., P. A., Mod. V (EC)
    (2) Haydn: String quartet, Op. 20, No. 5, second movement, mm. 1-17, Cad. H., P. A., Mod. III (EC)
    (3) Haydn: String quartet, Op. 74, No. 3, second movement, mm. 1-10, Cad. H., P. A., Mod. V
  D. Concertos and symphonic music:
    (1) Mozart: Piano Concerto No. 24 in C minor, K. 491, first movement, mm. 13-28, Cad. H., (EC) (involves Neapolitan sixth also)
    (2) Beethoven: Symphony No. 5, second movement, mm. 72-80, Cad. P. A.
    (3) Brahms: Symphony No. 1, second movement, mm. 1-4, Cad. H.
    (4) Tschaikovsky: Symphony No. 6, first movement, mm. 1-6, Cad H.

4. The French sixth chord
  A. From the 371 Chorales of Bach:
    (1) No. 146, mm. 1-5, Cad. H., P. A. (EC)
  B. Piano music:
    (1) Franck: *Prelude, Aria and Finale* for Piano, Prelude, mm. 1-13, Cad. I. A., H. (EC) (involves German sixth also)

    (2) Chopin: Prelude, Op. 28, No. 20, mm. 9-12, Cad. P. A. (involves Neapolitan chord also)

    (3) Schubert: Moment Musical, Op. 94, No. 6, mm. 1-16, Cad. H., P. A. (EC)

C. Chamber music:

    (1) Beethoven: Trio, Op. 97, "Archduke," third movement, mm. 1-8, Cad. P. A., Mod. V (EC)

    (2) Beethoven: String Quartet, Op. 59, No. 3, mm. 1-24, Cad. H. (EC) (this passage provides excellent drill in identification of seventh chord types)

D. Symphonic music:

    (1) Beethoven: Symphony No. 3, first movement, mm. 15-23, Cad. H. (EC)

    (2) Brahms: Symphony No. 4, fourth movement, mm. 1-4, Cad. P (EC)

ALTERED CHORD FUNCTION

(1) (Given: Soprano, D♯ or E♭; Bass, F)

(2) (Given: Soprano, C♯ or D♭; Bass, E♭)

(3) (Given: Soprano, C or B♯; Bass, D)

EXCERPTS FROM LITERATURE

1. NEAPOLITAN SIXTH CHORD

Chopin: Mazurka, Op. 63, No. 2

Haydn: Symphony No. 104 in D major, first movement

2. ITALIAN SIXTH CHORD

Purcell: *Dido and Aeneas*, "Thy Hand, Belinda"

A L T E R E D   C H O R D S · **235**

Adagio Lamentoso

Tschaikovsky: Symphony No. 6 in B minor, fourth movement

3. GERMAN SIXTH CHORD

Larghetto

Mozart: *Requiem,* "Lachrymosa"

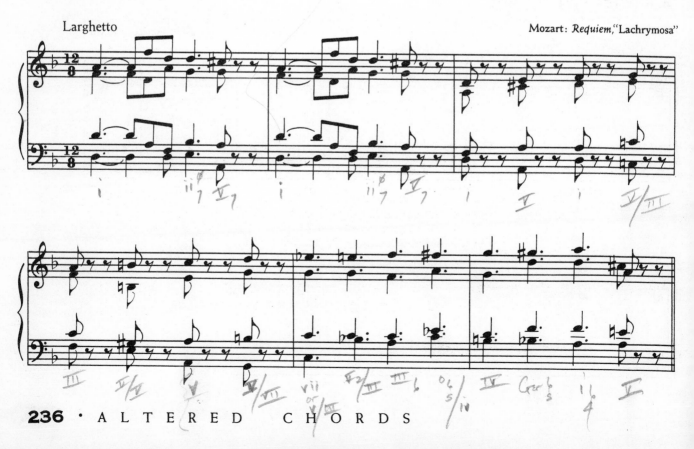

Allegretto   Mozart: String Quartet in D minor, K. 421, third movement

4. FRENCH SIXTH CHORD

Grave   Handel: *Messiah*, "Since By Man Came Death"

Allegro   Beethoven: Sonata in C minor, Op. 13, third movement

A L T E R E D   C H O R D S · **237**

Sight singing

LIST OF SIGHT SINGING FROM LITERATURE

(1) Mozart: *Requiem Mass*, No. 8, Lachrymosa
(2) Verdi: *Requiem*, Libera Me, mm. 132-170 (with solo)
(3) Mendelssohn: *Elijah*, No. 1, "Help Lord"

EXCERPTS FROM LITERATURE

Mozart: Twelfth Mass, "Gloria"

Allegro moderato

Schubert: *Mass in G,* "Sanctus"

Adagio maestoso